Active Investing Wealth Management
for
High Net Worth Individuals

An Educational Book

Active Investing Wealth Management for High Net Worth Individuals

Specifically designed for High Net Worth Individuals
with $1 million or more of investable assets

Your "How-to" Guide to:
Go Beyond Common Portfolio Management Practices

危機

Danger + Opportunity = Risk

By

Dr. Gary J. Harloff, Ph.D.
Harloff Capital Management
Registered Investment Advisory Firm
<*www.harloffcapital.com*>
440-871-7278

Copyright © 2007, 2008, 2010 by Harloff Inc.

Library of Congress Control Number:		2009911436
ISBN:	Hardcover	978-1-4415-9390-0
	Softcover	978-1-4415-9389-4
	EBook	978-1-4500-0378-0

Copyright 2007, 2008, 2010 by Harloff Inc. All rights reserved. No part of this publication may be copied, distributed, transmitted, transcribed, stored in a retrieval system, transferred in any form or by any means, electronic, mechanical, magnetic, manual, or otherwise, or disclosed to third parties without the express written permission of Harloff Inc., 26106 Tallwood Drive, North Olmsted, OH 44070 U.S.A., 440-871-7278, <www.harloffcapital.com>.

The purpose of this scholarly book is to teach individuals and students about wealth management and investing. It is realized that the book will have limited sales and may be a profitless educational book. Substantial research has been conducted to review the investing literature to determine the state-of—the-art. Various factual (not creative) investment concepts are commented upon, quoted from, explained, criticized, and reported from data, figures, and tables from the cited literature. This book employs only a small portion, in relation to the whole, of any of the original referenced sources. This book does not compete with (take away sales from) the cited literature. The effect of this *fair use* upon the potential market or value of the referenced sources is negligible.

The information presented and any opinion expressed is to not be considered a solicitation to purchase or sell any security or any service. The information contained in this workbook is not intended to be tax, legal, or financial advice. You are encouraged to seek advice from your own financial and tax counselors, as qualified advisors should always be consulted before acting on any financial, legal and tax matters. The content is developed from sources believed to be correct and are not guaranteed. Harloff Inc. assumes no responsibility for statements made in this publication including, but not limited to, typographical errors or omissions, statements regarding legal, tax, or investment matters.

Disclosure: The book does not report any money manager's actual results. These results are not to imply, or a reader should not infer from them, anything about the writer's investment competence or about future investment results. Disclosures include: material market or economic conditions are portrayed where appropriate by indicating S&P500 and NDX100 index results with the hypothetical portfolio results; hypothetical results are not managed and do not reflect the deduction of any advisory fees, brokerage or other commissions and any other expenses that a client would have paid or actually paid; the reinvestment of dividends and other earnings may be or may not be accounted for in the hypothetical transactions, however the S&P500 and NDX100 indexes do not reflect dividends and other earnings and an investor may not directly invest in these two indexes; the potential for profit has the potential for loss; individual funds, indexes, investments, and hypothetical results all have different volatility; hypothetical portfolio contains investments that are selected with a view towards capital appreciation; hypothetical results do not represent actual trading and may not reflect the impact that material economic and market factors might have had on the writer's decision-making if the writer were actually managing clients' money; it is possible that conditions, objectives, or investment strategies of the hypothetical portfolio may have changed materially during the time portrayed and it is impossible to determine the effect of any such changes on the results portrayed; any of the securities contained in, or the investment strategies followed with respect to the hypothetical portfolios may not relate to the type of advisory services offered by the writer, e.g. the book may include some types of securities that the writer may no longer select for its clients; writer's actual clients may have had materially different investments and investment results from the hypothetical results. Money market interest not considered. Values in this book are believed to be correct, but are not guaranteed.

This book was printed in the United States of America.

To order additional copies of this book, contact:
Xlibris Corporation
1-888-795-4274
www.Xlibris.com
Orders@Xlibris.com

This book is dedicated to Eve Eacott, my daughter, whose interest and help in my portfolio management research is inspirational to me. And to Jessica Eacott, my granddaughter, who is a fighter.

Preface

"We cannot seek or attain health, wealth, learning, justice or kindness in general. Action is always specific, concrete, individualized, unique", by Benjamin Jowett (1817-1893).

Conventional wisdom suggests that individual investors accumulate investment gains best with a passive diversified portfolio "buy-and-hold" approach. Any yet, individual investor's average mutual fund compound annual return is about 9 % LESS THAN the S&P500 return over extended periods. And this is not counting initial commissions paid. For example, from 1984 to 2002 the average investor yearly mutual fund return is 2.57 % compared to 12.22 % for the S&P500. Similar underperformance holds for periods from 1984 to: 1997, 1998, 2000, and for 20-year periods ending in 2007 and 2008. Why do average investors under perform the market? The reasons for underperformance are discussed and more advanced strategies are reviewed.

This book provides an overview of the wealth management process and a comprehensive view of the investing process. This discussion should be of particular interest to high net worth investors who wish to go beyond the common buy-and-hold strategy. Taking a more informed and active role in one's investing wealth management process should be helpful in reaching financial goals.

Chapter Summaries

1. Overview of Wealth Management Process
On the wealth management process where the wealth manager is a coach who manages specialist professionals.

2. Overview of Investing
On the products and services of investing. Passive and active investing strategies, and market timing are introduced.

3. High Net Worth (HNW) Community Description
On the description, wants, and needs of high net worth investors.

4. Family Wealth Management
On family office description, goal setting, and accountability.

5. Classical and Tactical Asset Allocation Strategies
Comparison and contrast of buy-and-hold and active investment strategies.

6. Math of Investing
On total return, compound return, inflation effects, currency effects, alpha and beta definition, expected returns, and time variation of returns.

7. Portfolio Theory Examples
On the 1952 "modern portfolio theory" considerations, stock/bond ratio, and Buffet study.

8. Risk Evaluation
On risk tolerance evaluation.

9. Example Investment Proposal: Hypothetical Case Study
On a typical financial plan for a 47 year old.

10. Goals and Constraints
On goals and constraints that may impact a financial plan.

11. Example Investment Policy Statement
On investment objectives, wealth manager selection and duties, investment advisor duties, and example investment policy/financial plan.

12. Annotated Bibliography
On the academic literature baseline of the buy-and-hold concept in terms of: goals, constraints, risk evaluation, investment theory, asset allocation, and tax issues.

13. Summary and Conclusions
On the state of the art of wealth management, asset allocation, and market timing.

14. Appendix. Outline of Wealth Management Body of Knowledge
Presents an overview of the general knowledge base of CFA exam-pass designated wealth managers.

15. References
On the references employed.

Acknowledgements

I wish to acknowledge editorial help from E. Eacott and D. Harris.

CONTENTS

Preface 7
Chapter Summaries 9
1. Overview of Wealth Management Process 23
    Retirement Discussions 25
    Investment Strategy 25
    Business Succession Strategy 25
    Estate Distribution Strategy 26
    Insurance Strategy 26
2. Overview of Investing 26
    Standard Asset Classes 26
    Alternate Asset Classes 26
    Investment Products and Services 26
    Passive Investing 30
    Active Investing 32
    Market Timing 32
    Conventional Wisdom 33
    Investment Risks are Real 34
    Gains are Illusive for Some Investors 34
    The Average Mutual Fund Investor Gains About 9.2%/Year
        LESS THAN the S&P500 Yearly Return! 35
    Leading Indicator Effects on Stock Market 35
3. High Net Worth (HNW) Community Description 38
    Retirement Plans 41
    HNW Location and Growth Rate in the U.S. 42
    Canadian HNW Statistics 45
    How to Differentiate Investment Managers 49
    How a Wealth Manager Can Hurt Your Wealth 51
    Smaller Investment Firms May Offer Advantages Over
        Wire-House and Big Firms 52
    Portfolio Rebalance Frequency 52

4. Family Wealth Management 53
   Family Office 53
   Values and Goals 54
   Accountability 55
   Family Combined Resources 55
   Diversification 55
   Active Management 56
   How a Passive Trip-Advisor Can Ruin Your Journey 57
5. Classical and Tactical Asset Allocation Strategies 58
   Investment Processes: Classical: buy-and-hold 58
   Bear Market Effect on Investing 62
   Dynamic Asset Allocation 63
   Investment Processes: Tactical 63
   Historical Returns for Buy-and-Hold (Not Managed) 64
   Asset Class Performance Next Year is Not Last Year's Winner 64
6. Math of Investing 70
   Total Return 70
   Compound Return 70
   Inflation 71
   Foreign Investment and Currency Effect on Annual Returns 71
   Risk 72
   Portfolio Optimization 72
   Example of Portfolio Optimization 74
   Problems with Modern Portfolio Theory in 2000 Bear Market 75
   Trading Strategies 76
   Absolute and Relative Investing and Alpha and Beta 78
   Example of a Dynamic Asset Allocation Strategy 81
   Market Timing: the Best and Worst 10 days Over About 23 years .. 83
   Expected Returns 84
   Income Portfolio Example 85
   Tax Deferred Growth with a Variable or Fixed Annuity 86
   Example Return Variation Over Time 87
7. Portfolio Theory Examples 89
   Buffet Large Capitalization Growth Study 98

8. Risk Evaluation 99
    Logic or Emotion 99
    Story or Data...100
    Fear of Losing 100
    Estimate..100
    Small Samples...101
    Sample Risk Tolerance Questionnaire 101
9. Example Investment Proposal: Hypothetical Case Study.............105
10. Goals and Constraints 114
    Goals 114
    Constraints 115
11. Example Investment Policy Statement................................115
    Typical Plan Passive Allocations....................................119
12. Annotated Bibliography 121
    a. Private Wealth Management: Goals and Constraints 122
    b. Risk Evaluation of Private Investors 126
    c. Private Wealth Management and Modern Investment
        Theory..127
    d. Asset Allocation for Private Investors......................128
    e. Tax Investing Issues..134
13. Summary and Conclusions 136
14. Appendix. Outline of Wealth Management Body of Knowledge 138
15. References..139

Tables

Table 1. Brief Description of Strategies. 33
Table 2. S&P500 Index and the Average Investor Compound Return, % per Year. 35
Table 3. Business Cycle Leading Indicator Effect on US Stock Market; Positive 4. 37
Table 4. Performance for Harloff's The Intelligent Fund Investor Monthly Newsletter, Vol. 12, Year 16, December 2009. 38
Table 5. U.S. Metropolitan Areas with the Greatest Number of HNW Households, 2006. 42
Table 6. U.S. Metropolitan Areas with the Greatest Growth in HNW Households, 2003-2006. 43
Table 7. HNW Feel Wealthier in 2007. 44
Table 8. HNW Asset Types and %. 44
Table 9. Investment Decisions; Don't Add to 100%. 45
Table 10. Estimated Number of HNW Households. 45
Table 11. Source of Private Client Wealth. 46
Table 12. Wealth Controlled by HNW Individuals is Estimated to Grow at 8.6%/year. 46
Table 13. Deposit and Fixed Income Assets are Projected to Decline From 55% of Total in 2002 to 32% in 2007. 46
Table 14. HNW Individuals Have Four Relationship Styles. 47
Table 15. Private Client Households Using Investment Counselors, 2005. 47
Table 16. Institutions Serving Private Client. 47
Table 17. Private Client Use of Investment Counselors to Increase. 48
Table 18. Percentage of Affluent Wanting Financial Services (doesn't add to 100%). 48
Table 19. Typical Expected Returns and Objectives of Advisors. 48
Table 20. Types of Advisors. 49
Table 21. Advisor Business Models. 49
Table 22. Separately Managed Accounts. 50
Table 23. Results of Several Rebalancing Frequencies Over a 15-year Period. 53

Table 24. Comparison of Classical and Tactical Investment Processes: Classical or Tactical. 59
Table 25. Investment Process: Classical, buy-and-hold. 60
Table 26. Bear Market Losses and Years to Recover. 62
Table 27. Investment Process: Tactical. 63
Table 28. Annual Returns 1926-1994. 64
Table 29. Asset Class Index Performance Varies From Year-to-Year 1987-2006. 66
Table 30. Average Return and Risk for Asset Class Indexes, 1987-2006. 67
Table 31. Variation of Alpha and Beta of NDX vs. S&P500 for Three Time Periods. 80
Table 32. Dynamic Frontier Primary and Alternate Asset Class Pairs for a Preferred Dynamic Asset Allocation Strategy. 82
Table 33. Dynamic Asset Allocation Doesn't have to be Perfect to Beat Buy-and-Hold for S&P500 from 1/1/1980 to 12/31/2002. 84
Table 34. Income Portfolio Example for Ms. Smith. 85
Table 35. Several Bond and Stock Allocations for Ms. Smith. 85
Table 36. Tension Between Yield and Appreciation. 86
Table 37. Typical Client Presentation Graphic. 92
Table 38. Typical Historical Correlation Matrix. Data from 1970 to 2001. 93
Table 39. Example Asset Allocation Correlations. 93
Table 40. Description of 3 Efficient Portfolios. 94
Table 41. Description of Efficient Portfolios. 95
Table 42. Expected Return of Stock/Bond with Risk Corrections and With Added Asset Classes, 1993. 97
Table 43. Annual Performance Summary of Berkshire Hathaway Stock, Stock Portfolio and S&P500 Comparison, 1980 to 2003. 98
Table 44. Risk Tolerance Analysis. 106
Table 45. Proposed Asset Allocation. 109
Table 46. Forecast Asset Values. 110
Table 47. Plan Implementation. 113
Table 48. Example of Asset Allocation Policy for Fixed Income, $1. Million and Equity $1.3 Million. 119
Table 49. Example of MSCI World Index Weights. 120

Table 50. Summary Holdings of 91 Large Pension Plans,
    1974-1983. 122
Table 51. Annualized 10-Year Returns of Large Plans,
    1974-1983. 123
Table 52. Goodness of Fit Explained from Brinson et. al. 1986. 124
Table 53. College/University Endowments: 2003 Average Asset
    Allocation..133
Table 54. Additional Wealth From $10,000 Invested After
    Different Return and Tax Rates Applied. 135

Figures

Figure 1. Growth Trends in the Affluent and HNW Market. 41
Figure 2. 20 Year Return vs. Risk, 1987 to 2006 Yearly Asset
    Class Index Performance. 67
Figure 3. Perfect Timing Index $1. Grows to $50.64 Compared
    to $12.52 RU 2000 Value Buy-and-Hold, 1986-2006.
    Hypothetical No Fees. 68
Figure 4. Asset Allocation Weights for Optimal Timing Indexes,
    1987-2007. 69
Figure 5. Return and Risk Efficient Frontier. 75
Figure 6. Nasdaq 100 (Higher Line) and S&P500 (Lower Line)
    Prices From 2/3/1998 to 9/10/2007 76
Figure 7. Trading Strategy (Hypothetical) Showing
    $1.00 Growing to $5.25 for S&P500 Whereas
    Buy-and-Hold Grows to $1.51 from 2/2/1998 to 9/10/2007. 77
Figure 8. Trading Strategy (Hypothetical) Showing $1.00
    Growing to $41.11 for NDX Whereas Buy-and-Hold
    Drops to $0.93 from 2/2/1998 to 9/10/2007. 77
Figure 9. Nasdaq 100, NDX, Change vs. S&P500 Change
    Daily From 2/3/1998 to 9/10/2007 78
Figure 10. Daily Change of NDX vs. S&P500 During Bull
    Market From 12/31/1998 to 12/31/1998. 80
Figure 11. Daily Change of NDX vs. S&P500 During Bull
    market from 3/24/2000 to 10/9/2002. 81
Figure 12. Yearly Return vs. Monthly Volatility or Risk. 83
Figure 13. Example of Index Annuity. 87
Figure 14. Fifteen-Year Annual Compounded Return and Risk,
    Ending 6/30/1993. 88
Figure 15. Sample Portfolio Mean Monthly Return and
    Standard Deviation. 89
Figure 16. Optimized Portfolios Along Efficient Frontier, Mean
    and Monthly Standard Deviation. 90
Figure 17. Efficient Frontier for S&P500 and Russell 2000
    From 1946 to 2000. 91
Figure 18. Efficient Frontier With Many Asset Classes 96
Figure 19. Efficient Frontier and Three Risk Levels. 107
Figure 20. Proposed Asset Allocation Pie Chart. 108

Figure 21. Asset Mix Comparison. 109
Figure 22. Proposed Asset Allocation Pie Chart. 112
Figure 23. Fifteen-Year Annual Compounded Return and Risk
           for the Period Ending June 30, 1993. 125
Figure 24. Average Equity Weight vs. Average Bond Weight,
           1977-1987. 129
Figure 25. Average Return vs. Average Plan Risk, 1977-1987. 129
Figure 26. Cumulative Excess Return on a U.S. Stock/Bond
           Timing Strategy. 131
Figure 27. Pension Asset Allocation—TIAA-CREF Premium
           Paying and Paid-Up Participants. 132
Figure 28. College/University Endowment Asset Allocation. 133
Figure 29. Annual vs. Projected Equity Allocations—Equities
           and Bonds Only. 134

An Educational Book

Active Investing Wealth Management for High Net Worth Individuals

By

Dr. Gary J. Harloff, Ph.D.
Harloff Capital Management
Registered Investment Advisory Firm
<www.harloffcapital.com>
440-871-7278

Active Investing Wealth Management for High Net Worth Individuals

1. Overview of Wealth Management Process

This book presents the investing portion of wealth management in some detail and is specifically designed for high net worth (HNW) individuals of investable assets of at least $1 million excluding primary residence. Other important areas of wealth management are briefly discussed below.

Wealth management is a process and not a product that can be purchased. Generally, the wealth management process is to establish individual and family wealth goals, collect and analyze financial and personal data, establish a consensus between the HNW individual and professional specialists, implement the specialist's recommendations, and monitor the progress of the strategies. This process includes several components including: investment management, wealth transfer, and professional relationship management. Investment management includes husbanding existing wealth, and growing wealth through investing. Wealth transfer is the transferring of wealth according to the individual's desires. Professional relationship management includes coaching professionals who may have significant expertise beyond that of the coach or wealth manager. These professionals include: portfolio manager(s), insurance specialist(s), private client lawyer(s), corporate tax attorney(s), and estate lawyer(s).

A wealth manager's job is planning to assist a HNW individual in obtaining his or her goals. Wealth managers position themselves in the center of the professional relationship activities. Most wealth managers are generalists who gain the confidence of the individual. The roles of wealth manager and investment manager are sometimes confused because some wealth managers attempt to be both personal counselor and money manager. A money manager's job is to provide absolute portfolio return or in some cases relative portfolio return at an agreeable risk level, over an agreed upon time period. Because it is difficult for individuals to easily discern the investment experts from the sales force, clients may be receiving less expertise than they are paying for. For example, sales oriented wealth managers/investment advisors may spend less than 4 hours per year on their client's investment strategy, selection, and monitoring. Technology helps generalists appear to be specialists by enabling the commodity production of financial plans with color graphic charts and tables. Many of these charts and tables may have little meaning. Therefore some understanding of the wealth management process is helpful to HNW individuals to obtain the best help needed. The investment manager takes ownership of the investment results. This is an easy way to keep these two roles separate. The wealth manager provides the planning but is not the investment specialist who own's return and risk.

Where investment proposals are sought from CFP and CFA exam-pass designated advisors, in most cases, the proposals will be similar because the similar training and technology. Responding strategies are likely to be buy-and-hold a diversified "optimal asset allocation" until next year. Computerized templates are available that enable rapid and common response to proposal requests. This book discusses the underlying assumptions that lead to similar proposed investment plans. Other advanced strategies are also discussed herein.

Besides common buy-and-hold investment strategies, active money management strategies seek absolute performance. Active managers include mutual fund timers and hedge fund managers. These managers attempt to select allocations that are going up and avoid allocations that are going down. Changes in asset allocation can be large and sudden. Active strategies include changes in strategic (long term) allocations, tactical (short term) allocations, and possibly market timing. Market timing is as old as the Dow Theory, e.g. buy when transports and industrials both go up. Timing includes investing when market conditions are favorable and not investing when conditions are not favorable.

Retirement Discussions

Before retiring, it is good to discuss goals and wishes with a professional or family member to provide for a successful retirement path. Exploring different investment strategies and risk assessments are a part of this discussion. Most individuals are not equipped to go beyond a passive buy-and-hold investment approach.

Investment Strategy

Developing an investment strategy includes discussing: (a) absolute and relative return investment processes, (b) active and passive approaches, (c) liquid investment vehicles, e.g. stocks, mutual funds, ETFs, emerging markets, international markets, and bonds, and (d) how risk is managed.

Business Succession Strategy

Developing a business succession strategy involves deciding the issues of equity distribution, income distribution, and control. These are difficult issues because families and businesses change with time. Also tax laws are complex and change. Succession strategy includes:

- Obtaining an objective business evaluation
- For businesses above $100 million in sales, a succession advisory team may be needed
- Decrease business cost of capital and increase free cash flow to raise company valuation
- Strengthen management team so the company can succeed without you
- Sell your accounts receivable, reduced by a large percentage if necessary, to raise income.

Estate Distribution Strategy

Developing an estate distribution strategy includes deciding on: financial security requirements, transfer of assets, and wealth preservation for one's family. Both the dollar amount of wealth and the individual's wishes can lead to a multi-generational wealth transfer strategy. There are many trust options that can help preserve assets and minimize taxes, and some options provide charitable support. There are also pitfalls due to complex legal issues, tax issues, and family dynamics.

Insurance Strategy

Life insurance is one way to generate and transfer wealth to family members and others upon the death of the insured.

2. Overview of Investing

Standard Asset Classes

Standard investment asset classes include: cash, bonds, US equity, and international equity.

Alternate Asset Classes

In addition to the standard asset classes, there are other alternate asset classes that may have low correlations with traditional asset classes. These include: private equity, venture capital, real estate, commodities, and hedge funds. These asset classes might be included in a portfolio to raise return and lower risk due to low historical correlation with the S&P500 index. The veracity of low and constant correlations, between asset classes, is addressed later.

Investment Products and Services

Equity stock share certificates represent partial ownership in a corporation. Equity shares may be voting shares, but not always.

Bonds are debt obligations issued by a corporation, government, or municipality. Bonds are usually ahead of stocks in corporate safety. Bond prices move inverse to interest rates until the maturity date. In other words, when bond prices go up, bond yields go down. Lower interest rates lower dollar based asset returns, reduce foreign demand for dollars, and the dollar weakens compared to foreign currencies, all other things being equal.

Mutual Funds are publicly pooled funds where a mutual fund manager picks stocks for the fund. No one investor gets a preferential or different portfolio; the fund's portfolio manager manages everyone's money the same way. Many fund families have a complete suite of asset classes, to try to keep an investor's money within the fund family. Many funds restrict the number of times per year investors can buy and sell. Some funds charge redemption fees of 1 to 2%, to discourage active trading. Redemption fees are imposed when funds are sold before a minimum holding time.

Most fund managers are not paid to raise cash in down markets and do not attempt to preserve the mutual fund's capital in down markets, i.e. these funds are long only investments. Most funds are classified by their "style" like large growth, or small value, and attempt to provide a relative return and risk to their style reference. In 2007, the overall mutual fund market is about $10 trillion market and typical yearly expenses are 0.75% to 1.5%.

Financial planners and brokers help clients find and purchase suitable investments and assist them in building client portfolios. These advisors generally do not have their own track record and act between investors and different money managers including: mutual funds, private portfolio managers, hedge funds, insurance companies, etc. They usually sell the track record of the manager, i.e. mutual fund. The investment sold to investors might be stocks, mutual funds, wrap programs, managed accounts, or (illiquid) private partnerships.

Registered money management companies (registered investment advisors) provide day-to-day portfolio management for public or private portfolios. In the latter case most mutual funds can be purchased at the institutional level with no sales commissions and active portfolio management is possible. These portfolio or money managers have their own track records.

The sales force earn commissions typically from 3% to 8% each time they sell a mutual fund to a client. With these commissions there is no incentive for the sales force to manage a portfolio of funds, and investors are encouraged to keep, or buy-and-hold, the funds until the next review/sales meeting. The sales force is regulated by the NASD and include: stock brokers, commissioned financial planners, and commissioned financial advisors. Fee-based financial advisors are usually independent and can purchase funds outside their company's product offerings. Thus there are at least three ways to pay including for investment help:

1. Commission to buy a product
2. A fee to have a financial advisor help with periodic selection
3. A fee to have a private money manager manage your portfolio.

Fee-based money management is permitted through registered investment advisory companies, and specially licensed stock brokers who work for broker dealer companies.

Some fee-based financial advisors sell a fixed portfolio, or asset allocation, of funds that doesn't change over time or market conditions without any sales commissions. These advisors may also offer an asset allocation service to (slightly) reallocate the portfolios from once to four times per year. Generally, rebalancing involves selling winners and buying losers.

Other fee-based private money managers, registered investment advisor representatives, actively manage with discretion the mutual fund and index investments and attempt to add value in both up and down markets by changing the fund selection and asset allocation according to stock market changes. These managers spend a lot of time and effort analyzing the stock markets and know when markets move.

Privately managed accounts, separately managed accounts, and individually managed accounts are all the same thing. They are usually managed by fee-based registered investment advisor (RIA) representatives. Assets in these accounts are growing, e.g. from $161 billion in 1996 to $383 billion in 2003. (Source: Money Management Institute, 2003). Separately managed accounts have about $789 billion (Source: Money Management Institute, Investment News, October 29, 2007). These accounts can be either: (a) actively managed by independent money managers with a goal of capital appreciation in good markets and capital preservation in stressed markets, or (b) passively managed or simply sold to the individual until the next review meeting.

Privately managed accounts can: (1) be customized for individual clients, (2) provide for transparency where clients readily see their holdings, (3) provide access to quality management usually unknown to the public, and (4) provide for tax efficiency with loss harvesting. For actively managed strategies, institutional class shares can be bought and sold with no sales charges. Some index mutual funds have leverage and some have inverse funds. Inverse funds go up when the underlying index goes down. This enables investors to effectively take a short position in a retirement account (IRA, 403(b), or 401(k) account) by purchasing an inverse fund. These fund companies are usually "timer friendly", in that they permit active trading and don't charge early redemption fees.

Unified managed accounts (UMA) are professionally managed investment accounts that may include stocks, bonds, mutual funds, and exchange traded funds. UMA have about $39 billion dollars as of the end of June 2007. (Source: Money Management Institute, Investment News, October 29, 2007).

Exchange Traded Funds (ETFs) are unmanaged index funds that trade like stocks (minute by minute) with no trading restrictions or penalties. ETFs mimic sectors, indexes, country funds, etc. Some ETFs have leverage and some are inverse or short vs. the underlying index. With time, ETFs will be an increasing choice in 401(k) plans due to lower management fees than mutual funds charge. Total ETF expense ratios are about 0.2 to 0.7% compared to mutual fund management expenses of 0.75 to 1.50% per year. There are also tax-free muni ETFs available, e.g. see ticker "MUB". As of August 2007 there were about 546 funds with $507.11 billion in assets. (Source: Investment Company Institute, 2008).

Hedge funds are pooled investments also called alternate funds or limited partnerships. Most are actively managed, while some are passively managed. An example of passive management is a fund with REIT sub-prime mortgage paper. Portfolio risk is difficult to judge for any REIT or illiquid equity investment. Management fees are typically 1-2% and incentive fees are usually 20% of net yearly profits. Portfolio turnover is usually much higher for actively managed hedge funds than mutual funds to earn higher incentive fees.

Fund of hedge funds are pooled investments that invest in other hedge funds similar to mutual funds investing in stocks. This adds another layer of fees and another layer of "due diligence". Due diligence is an undefined process of evaluation and analysis.

Variable annuities are insurance company products with a small insurance rider that enable investors to buy a limited suite of mutual funds within a contract. They are not exempt from security regulations. (Source: U.S. Supreme Court in SEC v. Valic 359 U.S. 65 (1959)). Advantages include: tax deferred growth, tax-free switching, unlimited contributions, insurance or death benefit, and may be protected from creditors in certain states. Disadvantages include: an insurance company fee of about 0.5% per year, usually high initial commissions between 3% to 8%, same tax withdrawal penalty as an IRA (withdrawals prior to age 59 ½ years triggers a 10% tax penalty), and withdrawn funds are taxed as ordinary income instead of capital gains. There are a few insurance companies that offer annuities with no or little sales commissions that can be professionally managed.

Initial public offering (IPO) is where stock of a new company is sold to new shareholders. This is big business at large wire-houses due to high commissions. Because money centers and commission structures differ in NY, London, and Beijing, the business may be shifting away from NY. For example, IPO commissions may be 6% in NY, 4% in London, and 2% in Beijing.

Passive Investing

Passive investing may be associated with the sale of mutual funds by the commissioned sales force. Many financial planners are passive investors. Financial planners, stockbrokers, and wealth managers may play the role of team coach to a HNW investor. As such they are ultimately responsible for investment performance to a HNW individual. However many wealth managers, who function also the investment manager, try to disassociate themselves from the portfolio return to retain their job even when performance goes South. It is also common for these dual role wealth managers to provide excessive—even smothering services, to try to become a trusted "family member" to HNWs.

Many financial planners with Certified Financial Planning (CFP) and Certified Financial Advisor (CFA) exam-pass designations have been taught to be passive buy-and-hold investors and that frequent asset allocation adjustments (market timing) doesn't pay. The basis for this teaching is consistent with a sales oriented business model; and is reviewed in chapter 12. Annotated Bibliography.

The mutual fund industry is largely passively managed with modern portfolio theory concepts. In contrast, hedge funds and separately managed accounts are largely actively managed. Estimated dollars committed to these products are listed below.

- About 8,036 mutual funds have roughly $9.3 trillion under management
- About 1,000 global hedge funds have about $1.2 trillion under management
- Combined assets of separately managed accounts (SMA) and ETFs are about $1.12 trillion.
(SOURCE: SUNGUARD, "A PROFILE OF ASSET CLASSES AND INVESTMENTS", SUNGUARD BROKER AND INVESTMENT ADVISOR, 2006 VOL. 2, 6).

Mutual funds generally have a hard time beating the S&P500 index. For example in 1997 and 1998 only about 10% of mutual funds beat the S&P500. One reason for underperformance is that most fund managers have to stay in their "style box" and this limits their success to that of their style box success in any particular year. A particular style box, like large cap growth, is best in certain business cycle times, and this limits the funds out performance. Also, most mutual funds are always long and are limited by prospectus to stay long. Thus in stressed markets, funds are forced to take losses instead of going to cash or short. Further, funds have underlying expenses of about 1%, whereas the S&P500 index is unmanaged with no expenses. Of course indexes cannot be bought directly. (Source: Laderman, J.M., "Mutual Funds: Can Anybody Out There Beat the S&P500?", Business Week, Dec. 17, 1998). Over a 25-year period ending December 2004, only about 20% of mutual funds beat the average of the stocks in the fund's style box. (Source: A to Z Investments, <http://www.atozinvestments.com/mutual-fund-index.html>).

Thus wealth managers, financial planners, and investment advisors who buy-and-hold a portfolio of funds for clients are limited to buying an average of funds that may under perform the S&P500.

Active Investing

Fee-based or incentive-based money managers including private or separately managed accounts, and hedge funds may practice active investing.

The academic literature seems to support the proposition that buy-and-hold beats all strategies. However, some academic journals are not admitting active investing or market timing research papers into their archives because editorial gatekeepers are biased against market timing.

Market Timing

Market timing is both small and large adjustments in asset allocation. (Small once or twice yearly allocation adjustments for buy-and-hold are consistent with "fixed" allocations of MPT and are actually buy-and-hold). RIA fees are typically less than 1.5% per year for ordinary or common allocation services of infrequent buy-and-hold small allocation changes. Many buy-and-hold services also include sales and annual commissions.

Large adjustments in asset allocation are made to adjust the portfolio to up and/or down market conditions. The differences between small infrequent and large frequent adjustments are addressed herein. Money manager RIA firms typically charge from 1.5% to 3.0% per year for frequent/ large allocation changes with no sales commissions. These advisors usually have specialized active or tactical strategies.

Table 1 summarizes these different investment strategies.

Table 1. Brief Description of Strategies.

Passive	
	Sales commission: stocks and funds, NASD governed
	Fee-based: fiduciary
Active	
	Fee-based: fiduciary if RIA
	Hedge fund: not fiduciary if not RIA
Strategies	
	Absolute: hedge funds have absolute return incentives
	Relative: mutual fund have index bogie
	Asset allocation close to index bogie allocations
Long /short	
	Long only: mutual funds
	Long/short: fee-based RIA, hedge funds
	Leverage: fee-based RIA, hedge funds
Market time	
	Small allocation changes and infrequent: fee-based RIA
	Large allocation changes and often: fee-based RIA, hedge funds

Conventional Wisdom

There are many investing concepts that are rules of thumb. Some are listed below.

- Diversification is a way to reduce risk. Yet, studies show that 6 to 9 uncorrelated stocks provide adequate diversification. Diversified portfolios of mutual funds need fewer than 6 to 9 funds since each fund usually holds about 100 stocks.
- Bond yields usually compete with stock market prices. When yields go up, stock prices usually go down. At times of panic or uncertainty, when investors seek a temporary safe harbor, money usually flows from stocks to bonds.

- It is more important to be in the right sectors or counties than in the right stocks. This concept favors mutual funds, index funds, and ETFs compared to picking individual stocks.
- Price momentum tends to stay in motion until acted upon by forces. Those forces may include: exhaustion of buyers/sellers, change in interest rates and bond yields, change in sector earnings outlook, change in credit availability, change in sector or country growth rate outlook, change in price of oil, rumor, etc.
- Currency valuation affects commodity prices. For example, when the dollar goes down, oil and basic materials go up in dollar terms. Relative country interest rates affect the country's currency value. For example, a country with higher interest rates will have a higher relative currency value, with all other variables the same.
- You might outlive your assets. For example, a healthy 65-year-old man has a 24% chance of living to 90, and a healthy 65-year-old woman has a 35% chance of living to 90. (Source: <www.researchmag.com>, p. 32, Oct. 2007).
- One's stock allocation should be about 100-age, and bond allocation should be about one's age. This simple allocation ignores that statistically Americans live longer than previously, and that bonds return less than stocks.

Investment Risks are Real

Consider the loss of:

- -37.2% from 1973-1974 in the S&P500 index
- -41.7% in 20 year government bond total return minus coupon interest from 1977-1981.
  (Source: based on a hypothetical one-bond portfolio with an average maturity of 20 years from Michael Muyot, April 21, 2005, Oppenheimer presentation, "Fee-based 1").

Gains are Illusive for Some Investors

Consider:

- From January 1984 to December 2000 the S&500 gained 1,300. %

- While the average investor gained only 141. %.
  (Source: Muyot, M., "Fee-based 1", Oppenheimer Presentation, April 21, 2005, Source: Delbar Financial Services, S&P500 dividends always reinvested, can't directly buy index, no expenses. Dividends not always reinvested for self managed portfolios.).

The Average Mutual Fund Investor Gains About 9.2%/Year *LESS* THAN the S&P500 Yearly Return!

Several studies of average mutual fund investor compound returns are compared in Table 2 to the S&P500 compound returns for six time periods. These data do not include initial commissions paid. The average investor gains about 9.2%/year *LESS* than the S&P500 yearly return! For example, over a 19-year period ending in 2002 the yearly compound return for the S&P500 was 12.22%, while the average investor return was 2.57%. This lower return could be due to buying high and selling low, e.g. selling out too late when the market goes down and waiting too long to reinvest. Similar results are indicated for years ending in 1997, 1998, 2000, 2007, and 2008. These results suggest the average mutual fund investor needs professional money management help.

Table 2. S&P500 Index and the Average Investor Compound Return, % per Year.
(Data source: Dalbar Inc. Financial Services of Boston, MA, "Quantitative Analysis of Investor Behavior Study" 1997, 1998, 2000, 2003, 2008, 2009 updates).

	1984-1997	1984-1998	1984-2000	1984-2002	1987-2007	1998-2008
S&P500, %	17.1	17.9	16.29	12.22	11.8	8.35
Avg. investor, %	6.7	7.25	5.32	2.57	4.5	1.87
Avg. investor—S&P500	-10.4	-10.65	-10.97	-9.65	-7.3	-6.48

Leading Indicator Effects on Stock Market

Business cycle considerations may be helpful in investing since the stock market is a leading business cycle indicator. By monitoring several leading indicators one may gain insight into stock market trends. Harloff quantifies the effects on the stock market of several leading indicators including: money supply, yield curve slope, dollar index, price/earnings rate, BAA corporate bond yield, ten-year bond yield/inflation, and fed funds rate. For the October 2007 time period these factors are deemed to be favorable on the U.S. equity market, see Table 3.

Because the business cycle is important to investing results, Harloff and Eacott have nondimensionalized many of the previous business cycles in the US to compare them. (Source: Harloff, G.J., Eacott, E.E., "U.S. Business Cycle Math Quantification", Harloff Inc., <www.harloffcapital.com>, 4-14-09, *<http://www.scribd.com/doc/14851834/US-Business-Cycle-Math-Quantification>*).

Table 3. Business Cycle Leading Indicator Effect on US Stock Market; Positive 4.
(Source: Harloff, G.J., "Harloff Capital Management's Market Outlook", Harloff Inc., October 2007).

(1) Positive (+1): Change in MZM (money with zero maturity), (2nd quarter 2007) = 8.00 %/year and is more than the average long-term annual change rate of 6-7%. Increase in money growth rate increases liquidity and stock prices usually rise.

(2) Positive (+1): Yield curve slope (July 2007) is positive = 5.00% (10 year) -4.96% (3 months) and this indicates that Fed policy is slightly accommodative. This spread of +0.04% is less than the historic value of 1.5 to 2.0%. The ratio of the 10-year to the 3 months yield is 0.91 and this is less than the historic spread of 1.0 to 1.6. Currently 10 and 30-year yields are increasing.

(3) Negative (-1): Dollar index 104.063 (July 2007) is 4.13% lower compared to its value a year ago, 108.543 (July 2006). This is less than inflation of 2.38 % (208.028 (CPI 7-1-07) / 203.200 (CPI 7-1-06)).

(4) Positive (+1): S&P500 Price/Earnings is about 16.99 (Barrons 8-20-07). A bond valuation model indicates that the S&P500 P/E should be 20.88. This indicates that prices are about 23 % under value from a bond viewpoint. This under valuation can exist for several quarters.

(5) Neutral (0): Credit risk: BAA corporate bond yield, as of January 2007, divided by the 10 year bond rate is 6.66%/ 4.79 % = 1.39. The normal ratio is 1.2-1.5. Thus, BAA yields are in the normal range and thus credit risk is in the normal range.

(6) Positive (+1): 10 year bond yields divided by inflation is 4.79 %/2.38 = 2.01. This is higher than the normal range of 1.2 to 1.45. At the upper range, holding inflation constant at 2.38 % gives a hypothetical 10-year bond yield of 3.45 % and a projected P/E of 28.99, for a 71. % increase in equity prices.

(7) Positive (+1): Overnight Fed funds rate is 5.25 % (8-20-07). Dividing this value by the inflation rate of 2.38 % gives 2.21. Short-term rates are usually 1.5 times inflation, so Fed funds rates should go lower. Using the 1.5 factor gives a projected Fed funds rate of 3.57

Harloff also quantifies global stock market sectors and indexes with his Harloff Value Index, HVI, indicator in the monthly newsletter Harloff's The Intelligent Fund Investor", published monthly since 1993. HVI is a new quantitative index employed to manage portfolios. Example performance of three hypothetical newsletter mutual fund portfolios and indexes, are given in "Table 4." from the December 2009 issue.

Table 4. Performance for Harloff's The Intelligent Fund Investor Monthly Newsletter, Vol. 12, Year 16, December 2009.
(Source: Harloff Inc., "Harloff's The Intelligent Fund Investor" Monthly Newsletter, Vol. 12, Year 16, December 2009).

Portfolio Performance, 2009 YTD, %

Ave of three portfolios	**(-11.54 % 2008) 54.49**
Dynamic frontier portfolio	(-3.20 % 2008) 56.65
No-Load agg growth portfolio	(-0.45 % 2008) 46.05
Rydex portfolio	(-30.97 % 2008) 60.77

Index Performance, YTD, %

S&P500 index.2009	(-38.49 % 2008) 22.06
NDX100 index.2009	(-41.89 % 2008) 49.17

Newsletter performance disclosure is on page 4. Portfolio performance is hypothetical in real time. Newsletter portfolio performance is without management fees or expenses. Index performance without management fees or dividends. One cannot directly invest in these indexes. Past performance does not insure future performance.

3. High Net Worth (HNW) Community Description

A description of the HNW community is presented from past surveys. Different surveys may provide different results.

There are about 2,000 U.S. households with assets of more than $100 million each. Many of these households have multiple homes with some outside the U.S. (Source: Boston Consulting Group, reported by Barrons, October 22, 2007, 34).

There are about 1.14 million U.S. households with a net worth, excluding primary residences, of $5 million or more. (Source: Spectrem Group, see Barrons, November 12, 2007, 34).

High Net Worth individuals have investable assets greater than $1 million (excluding primary residences). Households of HNW nearly doubled in past decade to 9.3 million, and represent 8 % of all US households. (Source: Zultowski, W.H., Phoenix High-Net Worth Market Insights, May 2007).

High Net Worth individuals include 5 to 6 million households, or the top 5% households, and control about $13 to14 trillion or 58.1% of the total U. S. financial assets. (Source: Spectrem Group and the Federal Reserve Board, 2001 Survey of Consumer Finances, with estimated growth through 2005. Reported in Oppenheimer Client Connect, June 15, 2005).

The younger "generation-X" (born 1965 or later) HNW group tends to be more bearish than the older group. Less than 1/3 are very or fairly optimistic about the economy for the next 1 to 2 years. (Source: Zultowski, W.H, Phoenix High Net Worth Market Insights, June 2007). Their concerns include:

- Bear market or recession effects on their wealth
- Retiring without a traditional retirement (investment or asset allocation) plan
- Social Security not being there when they need it
- Expect to support 1 or more aging parent(s)
- Expect to live longer than previous generations.

Business owners make up about 21% of all HNW households and have either private businesses or professional practice. (Source: LIMRA international "Financial Situation of the Affluent", 2002).

In Latin America there are about 300,000 high net worth individuals with over $3.8 trillion in assets. (Source: Opal Financial Group, 2007, <http://

www.opalgroup.net/conferencehtml/2007/latin_private_wealth07/latin_am_private_wealth.php>).

The affluent group is about 14.7 million U.S. households and represents 13% of all U.S. households. They have $500,000 to $1,000,000. in investable assets, and have a median age of 54. (Source: Zultowski, W.H, Phoenix High-Net Worth Market Insights, May 2007).

Wealthy clients may need:

- Cash management services
- Corporate lending products
- Investment banking when they sell their business.

Large bank wealth management teams can be helpful when special introductory services are needed to: government officials, regulators, or private equity investors. Bank clients sometimes end up paying extra fees that are hard to identify like $3,000 to $20,000 in "bank-integration-reporting" fees. At large banks, it is not uncommon for wealth managers, with clients having greater than $50 million in investable assets, to have only 10 clients.

Other services provided by non-banks, RIA, and legal firms include: investment management, estate planning, trust, and charitable trust creation.

Economic business and investment cycles affect the number of both HNW and affluent households. These households cycle with the U.S. economy, as is illustrated below in Figure 1. Business cycles have a bigger effect on the affluent, as the HNW households tend to be more diversified. For reference, a stock market bear market lasted from 2000 to 2003.

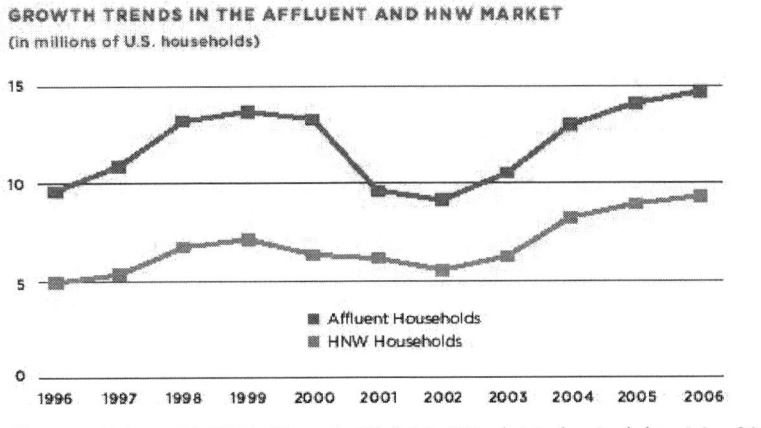

GROWTH TRENDS IN THE AFFLUENT AND HNW MARKET
(in millions of U.S. households)

[Chart showing Affluent Households and HNW Households from 1996 to 2006]

(Source: Zultowski, W.H., Phoenix High Net Worth Market Insights, May 2007).

Figure 1. Growth Trends in the Affluent and HNW Market.

The bull market of the 1990's helped some HNW investors overestimate their investment skills. Consider that even Nobel laureates with Long Term Capital were flummoxed by the Russian bond default. Principals lost $100's of millions. Their losses even threatened the US financial system 19 months before the bear market started in March 2000.

Retirement Plans

Many HNW individuals don't plan to retire, and will work part time. Others, up to 40% of those still working, do plan to retire. A common goal is to maintain their current comfortable standard of living.

For retirement income, some advisors say 80% of peak earning income is needed while 47% of those HNW surveyed believe they will need 100% of their peak earning income. Most are unlikely to own fixed or variable annuities or long term care insurance and less than 15% of those surveyed have annuities. Many are more optimistic about their financial well being than in the recent past. In late 1990's positive high returns were more important than capital preservation. However, in the bear market from 2000 to 2003, capital preservation was more important. In 2007 both high return and capital preservations are equally important goals. (Source: Zultowski, W.H., "The 2007 Wealth Survey", (Based on 1,800 interviews with individuals greater than 1 million, not counting primary residence. Sampling error +-2.3%.) reported in Phoenix High-Net Worth Market Insights, June 2007).

HNW Location and Growth Rate in the U.S.

New York, N.Y. has the largest concentration of HNW households; possibly because it is the financial capital of the world, see Table 5.

Table 5. U.S. Metropolitan Areas with the Greatest Number of HNW Households, 2006. (Source: 2000 Census, <www.census.gov/main/www/cen2000>, reported by Zultowski, W.H., Phoenix High-Net Worth Market Insights, May 2007).

U.S. Metropolitan Areas with the Greatest Number of HNW Households, 2006

Metro Area	Estimated number of HNW Households
New York	708,696
Los Angeles-Long Beach-Santa Ana	384,293
Chicago-Naperville-Joliet	327,994
Washington-Arlington-Alexandria	257,867
Philadelphia-Camden-Wilmington	221,074
San Francisco-Oakland-Fremont	191,905
Miami-Fort Lauderdale-Miami Beach	190,020
Boston-Cambridge-Quincy	182,640
Dallas-Fort Worth-Arlington	171,216
Detroit-Warren-Livonia	168,204
Houston-Sugar Land-Baytown	151,647
Atlanta-Sandy Springs-Marietta	148,399
Phoenix-Mesa-Scottsdale	120,366
Minneapolis-St. Paul-Bloomington	116,146
Seattle-Tacoma-Bellevue	113,342
Baltimore-Towson	105,219
San Diego-Carlsbad-San Marcos	102,138
Riverside-San Bernardino-Ontario	94,799
St. Louis	93,998
Tampa-St. Petersburg-Clearwater	87,326

Source: TNS Affluent Market Research Program, 2006

Estimated number of HNW households, with the greatest growth for several U.S. metropolitan areas are listed in Table 6. Poughkeepsie, NY is the fastest growing HNW household metro area in the U.S.

Table 6. U.S. Metropolitan Areas with the Greatest Growth in HNW Households, 2003-2006.
(Source: 2000 Census, <www.census.gov/main/www/cen2000>, reported by Zultowski, W.H., Phoenix High Net Worth Market Insights, May 2007).

U.S. Metropolitan Areas with the Greatest Growth in HNW Households, 2003-2006

Metro Area	Estimated number of HNW Households	Estimated Annualized Growth Rate (2003-2006)
Poughkeepsie-Newburgh-Middletown, NY	22,700	46%
Hagerstown-Martinsburg, MD-WV	6,219	41%
Portland-South Portland-Biddeford, ME	16,092	41%
Asheville, NC	12,004	38%
Florence, SC	4,518	34%
Waterloo-Cedar Falls, IA	4,332	29%
Jonesboro, AR	2,186	28%
Fort Smith, AR-OK	5,643	27%
Los Angeles-Long Beach-Santa Ana, CA	376,099	27%
Rapid City, SD	2,856	27%
Bloomington, IN	4,436	27%
Victoria, TX	2,878	26%
Rochester, MN	5,906	26%
Green Bay, WI	7,720	25%
Pine Bluff, AR	2,178	25%
Anchorage, AK	11,878	25%
Albany, GA	3,585	25%
Owensboro, KY	2,634	25%
Clarksville, TN-KY	4,244	24%
College Station-Bryan, TX	4,197	24%

Source: TNS Affluent Market Research Program, 2006

Many HNW households feel wealthier in 2007 than in 2006, see Table 7.

Table 7. HNW Feel Wealthier in 2007.
(Source: Zultowski, W. H., "Phoenix High-Net Worth Market Insights", June 2007).

- 81% feel wealthier than last year
- 45% feel their long-term wealth is "extremely secure"
- 33% don't have a primary advisor
- Younger millionaires are more uncertain of traditional pension plans
- First time in 6 years, return of assets is equally important as return on assets
- More want to match or exceed current income
- Fewer expect to ever retire
- Majority lack a written financial plan.

The HNW holdings in billions and % of total holdings are listed in Table 8.

Table 8. HNW Asset Types and %.
(Source: Zultowski, W. H., "Phoenix High-Net Worth Market Insights", June 2007).

	$ Billions holdings	*U.S. holdings* % of total
All financial assets	$11,812	58.1%
Stocks	3,424	78.2
Bonds	804	87.0
Personal ret plans[1]	2,446	42.7
Managed accounts[2]	1,646	74.5
Mutual funds (non-money market)	1,503	60.7

1) Includes 401(k) plans
2) Includes annuities trusts and managed accounts
(data Source: Federal Reserve Board, "Survey of Consumer Finances", 2001).

Many HNW investors switch advisors each year for a variety of reasons listed in Table 9.

Table 9. Investment Decisions; Don't Add to 100%.
(Source: Zultowski, W. H., "Phoenix High-Net Worth Market Insights", June 2007).

- 44%   Switch advisors because of lack of proactive contact
- 33%   Don't have a primary financial advisor
- 32%   Switch for lower returns than expected
- 25%   Receive advice from full service (commissioned) broker
- 24%   Switch because advisor is not offering the right products and services
- 14%   Admit they know little about making investments
- 7 to17%   Plan to look for new financial advisor this year
- 10%   Invest online or with discount broker.

Canadian HNW Statistics

Several characteristics of HNW investors are gleaned from a Canadian study. (Source: Sjögren, K. H., "Overview and Trends in the Wealth Management Business", Investor Economics, January 25, 2007. Presented by CFA Institute, <www.cfawebcasts.org>).

The number of HNW households in Canada are listed in Table 10.

Table 10. Estimated Number of HNW Households.

Emerging Wealthy ($1-$5 MM)	335,000
Wealthy ($5-$10MM)	60,000
Ultra Wealthy (greater than $10MM)	20,000

(Data source: Investor Economics Institute Analysis)

Sources of private wealth are listed in Table 11.

Table 11. Source of Private Client Wealth.
(Source: Sjögren, K. H., "Overview and Trends in the Wealth Management Business", Investor Economics, CFA Institute, January 25, 2007, <www.cfawebcasts.org>).

	Global	North America
Sale of business	37%	26%
Income	24	32
Inheritance	18	16
Investments	12	11
Restricted stock options	9	15

The wealth controlled by HNW individuals is estimated to grow at 8.6% per year, see Table 12.

Table 12. Wealth Controlled by HNW Individuals is Estimated to Grow at 8.6%/year.
(Source: Investor Economics Institute Analysis).

2004	$1,046 billion
2009	1,545
2014	2,391

Equities are estimated to equal deposits plus fixed income allocation in 2007, see Table 13.

Table 13. Deposit and Fixed Income Assets are Projected to Decline From 55% of Total in 2002 to 32% in 2007.
(Source: World Wealth Report, 2006).

Year	2002	2005	2007
Deposits	25%	13%	11%
Fixed Income	30	21	21
Equities	20	30	31
Alternative investments	10	20	22
Real Estate	15	16	15

HNW individuals have at least four relationship styles as indicated in Table 14.

Table 14. HNW Individuals Have Four Relationship Styles.
(Data Source: Sjögren, K. H., "Overview and Trends in the Wealth Management Business", Investor Economics, CFA Institute, January 25, 2007, <*www.cfawebcasts.org*>).

		2005	*2014*
1.	Delegators: need insurance; follow instructions	32%	25%
2.	Partners: how to allocate; decision between us	35	38
3.	Validators: this is what I believe-what do you think?	20	23
4.	Soloists: I will do it alone	13	14

The primary advisor is important to the HNW individual, yet it may not be clear who that person is. They are the first person called with a financial question. It might be a registered investment advisor (a fiduciary), a full service broker (not a fiduciary in general), an accountant, or a lawyer.

About 34% of HNW households use investment counselors, see Table 15.

Table 15. Private Client Households Using Investment Counselors, 2005.
(Source: Investor Economics, 2005).

- HNW households, total — 415,000
- HNW households that use investment counselors — 141,100 (34%)
- HNW households that use counselors as primary advisor — 91,300 (22%)

There are many institutions serving HNW individuals as listed in Table 16.

Table 16. Institutions Serving Private Client.
(Source: Sjögren, K.H., "Overview and Trends in the Wealth Management Business", Investor Economics, CFA Institute, January 25, 2007, <*www.cfawebcasts.org*>).

- Boutique RIA money manager and/or advisor
- International private banking
- Private wealth/investment counselor
- Multi-family office
- Private trust company/officer
- Private wealth manager (financial planner)
- Private client brokerage (stock broker).

HNW individuals are expected to increase their employment of investment counselors over the next several years, see Table 17.

Table 17. Private Client Use of Investment Counselors to Increase.
(Source: Canadian Millionaires Report).

Private client use of investment counselors who offer new products and strategies is expected to increase, as use decreases from financial planners and full service brokers.

2000   27%
2005   34
2014   37

Table 18 indicates that wealth management portfolio management strategies are most important to HNW individuals.

Table 18. Percentage of Affluent Wanting Financial Services (doesn't add to 100%).
(Source: Canadian Millionaires Report).

20%   Asset allocation
18   Fund selection
15   Financial plan
13   Tax preparation
12   Estate plan/trust
10   Insurance

Expected investment returns seem to be different for different groups of investors, financial planners, and active money managers, see Table 19.

Table 19. Typical Expected Returns and Objectives of Advisors.

Investors	Typical objective returns
Individuals	obtain 9.24%/year LESS THAN the S&P500 returns
Passive financial planners	about 90% of S&P500 (manage expectations lower)
Active money managers	same or greater than S&P500 with less risk

How to Differentiate Investment Managers

There are many investment advisors; some are fiduciaries who must put the HNW individual's interest ahead of their own. Those who are not fiduciaries may have a conflict of interest. Table 20 lists the percentage of various types of advisors.

Table 20. Types of Advisors.
(Source: "Cultivating the Affluent Newsletter", Charter Financial Publishing Network, October 2007).

25.5% Independent stock broker representatives—product sales, **not fiduciaries**
22.6 Insurance agents—product sales, **not fiduciaries**
19.5 Wire house and regional representatives—product sales, **not fiduciaries**
12.1 Registered investment advisors (RIA)—fee-based; don't sell products, manage money, **fiduciaries**
11.4 Private bankers/trust officers—**fiduciaries**
8.9 Property & casualty brokers—product sales, **not fiduciaries.**

Just as there are many types of advisors, there are also many advisor business models, see Table 21.

Table 21. Advisor Business Models.
(Source: "Cultivating the Affluent Newsletter", Charter Financial Publishing Network, October 2007).

48.9% Generalists
28.3 Wealth managers including: counselors, fee-based RIA, and financial planners
17.1 Product specialists including stock and insurance brokers
5.5 Multifamily offices.

Hedge fund managers are not fiduciaries unless they are registered as investment advisors and have oversight.

Separately managed accounts are wrap programs with individual stock or mutual fund portfolios. Individuals own securities in their managed account. These accounts are usually aimed at institutional investors and some have $100 million minimum. Attributes are listed in Table 22.

Table 22. Separately Managed Accounts.
(Source: Money Management Institute, FRC, press release February 1, 2005, see Advisor Custom Publishing, Investment Advisor Magazine, August 2005).

- $576.1 Billion at end of 2004
- 15.9% Increase over end of 2003.

Large brokerage houses have private client groups that provide (lots of) personal services. They provide opportunities to trade assets and purchase IPOs. They may be focused on transaction commissions with internal and external products and may have a conflict of interest. Stock brokers are governed by the NASD and are no longer allowed to provide fee-based brokerage money management, unless specially licensed to do so.

Trust bank services. The Glass-Steagall Act of 1933 prevented banks from brokerage business and this prohibition was repealed in 1999. Today banks set up and manage trusts for private clients usually with a conservative approach.

A list of differentiators of wealth management providers includes:

- Passive allocators, tend to buy-and-hold.—sales oriented
- Active allocators tend to actively reallocate
- Stock selector—needs 7 to 9 uncorrelated stocks for a diversified portfolio, stocks are quite volatile with daily price changes of 10 to 30% not uncommon
- Fund selector—need fewer than 7 uncorrelated funds for a diversified portfolio
- Commission product base. Sells company products to clients.—sales oriented
- Fee-based independent money management strategy.
- Mutual fund investing
- Alternative asset (hedge fund) investing
- Long only—sales oriented
- Long and/or short

- Always invested—sales oriented
- Market timing, i.e. changing asset weights to adjust portfolio to either rebalance portfolio or to adjust portfolio to market conditions
- Invest long in good market and in money market or short in bad market
- Employ 3, 5, or 20 years of old data in portfolio optimizer
- Employ data less than one year in portfolio optimizer
- Don't know how to compute alpha and beta—sales oriented
- Know how to compute alpha and beta
- Know how to invest short in a retirement account or IRA
- Passion for money management
- Passion for client and their family relationship.

With 1 to 2% management fee and 20% incentive fee, fund of funds managers add another 1% to 2% management and 20% incentive fee on top of the original hedge fund's fees.

How a Wealth Manager Can Hurt Your Wealth

Today, many wealth managers and financial planners set low investment return goal of 6-9% partly to:

- Lower client expectations so client won't quit a buy-and-hold program
- Lower goal may be consistent with less money management effort
- Align goal to be consistent with a buy-and-hold program.

Many wealth managers don't have a money management strategy beyond buy-and-hold, i.e. a static never-change asset allocation. This process sells winners to buy losers once or twice a year to get the portfolio asset allocation back in line with the initial asset allocation selected.

Questions to ask your wealth manager (WM):

- On what basis will you select my portfolio manager(s)?
- My WM will select my portfolio manager by _____.
- How will you meet my investment expectations?

- My WM's approach is _____.
- What is the basis for my trust of my WM?
- I trust my WM because _____.
- How will you add value for me?
- My WM adds value by _____.
- Is my WM's strategy common or special?
- My WM's strategy is _____ because _____.
- Do you know your present rate of return for all your equity and bond portfolios?
- My WM's rate of return for all his/her investments is _____ and it is ____ acceptable.
- Do you know your cost of fees, commissions, and expenses?
- My WM's costs are $_____ fees, $_____ commissions, and $_____ expenses.
- What is your overall trust level of your WM?
- My overall trust level with my WM is _____.

Smaller Investment Firms May Offer Advantages Over Wire-House and Big Firms

Innovation and new investment technology comes from individuals, intelligence, and hard work. Yet many small or emerging managers are routinely screened out due to their small size, rather than for their investment expertise. Boutique shops are not able to advertise as effectively as large Wall Street firms. The "pay for play" practice of some institutions also restricts accessible talent.

Portfolio Rebalance Frequency

Table 23 illustrates that the average yearly return over 15 years, drops with increasing rebalance frequency. Each rebalance commission cost is $126. One might conclude that rebalancing can't beat buy-and-hold when commissions are paid. But commissions have dropped considerably since this study and many RIA managed programs are without commissions.

Table 23. Results of Several Rebalancing Frequencies Over a 15-year Period.
(Source: Stine, B., and Lewis, J., "Guidelines for Rebalancing Passive-investment Portfolios", Journal Financial Planning, April 1992, 80-86).

Rebalancing Strategy	holding period return, %	no. of times rebalance	commission costs $
Buy & hold	7.54	0	0
Annual	6.79	15	2,201
Semiannual	6.69	30	4,088
Quarterly	6.47	60	7,560

Many financial planners recommend semiannual or yearly portfolio rebalance, independent of what the market is doing. This process sells winners to buy losers to keep the allocation constant and is not attuned to business cycle changes and changing optimal asset allocations.

How often should my portfolio be rebalanced and why? _____

To determine if you believe in the buy-and-hold fixed asset allocation process, ask yourself if your portfolio should be the same in a bear market as it is in a bull market? If you believe your portfolio should be different, then you believe in active management.

4. Family Wealth Management

Family Office

There are a few thousand family offices in the US. They coordinate administration and investments of one or several family's financial assets. Offices also do tax, legal work, and bookkeeping. Family offices usually oversee $50 million to billions to be competitive. Some offices plan for multigenerational wealth: preservation, growth, and transfer.

Family offices might retard individual family member development by: helping too much and taking financial responsibility away from the wealth owner.

Sometimes, the office is not able to compete for top money management talent.

Family wealth management begins by setting: family goals, family buy-in with accountability plans, and establishing a vision for an investment process. Helpful questions are listed below.

Values and Goals

Family value and goal articulation is needed for effective family wealth management. Information needed includes: family goals, family assets, spending patterns, expected rates of return, acceptable risk, and estate plans. It is helpful to write down issues.

Define family long-term goals:

My family's primary long-term goals is: _____

My family's primary financial goal is: _____

Forces that might work against me include: low returns, fees, taxes, and inflation.

These forces work against me by: _____

To alter these forces I can: _____

Disciplined family leadership is needed for long-term family wealth management.

The number of generations I am planning for is: _____

A comprehensive strategy is very important and includes reasons to work together.

My strategy is: _____

Accountability

Wealth management is a business where accountability metrics are employed. Quantifying progress is needed to judge performance of family office advisors including: wealth manager, money managers, accountants, and lawyers, etc.

My accountability metrics include:_____.

I need to measure overall investment return. Overall performance measurements is needed due to multiple custodians, investment advisors, and illiquid assets.

My performance metric is: _____.

Family Combined Resources

Family resources are diverse and change over time.

Family combined resources are: _____.

Encourage family members to work together in activities, discussions, and meetings.

New ways my family can work together are: _____.

Delegate aspects of wealth management to your professional team as much as possible and empower them.

Delegated tasks include: _____.

Delegated people include: _____.

Diversification

Diversifying investments is one way to lower risk. Diversification includes investing in different asset classes like: health care, basic materials, bonds, real estate, emerging countries, precious metals, etc. Risk can be spread out and hopefully when return in one asset class goes down return in another asset class goes up. Active management is another way to manage risk.

I need more/less diversification in: _____

Tax rates vary and depend on investments and ownership. Stock prices, capital gains, tax-deferred investments, and trust ownership are examples of this.

My portfolio includes different taxable investments of: _____

It is important to measure my wealth management team's skill. What might happen if a particular member leaves?

My bench is shallow in: _____

Active Management

Active management is natural in you daily life. You manage your family, education, your job, and company. Many planners often overlook active focused management of investments. Active investment management may serve you better than common passive buy-and-hold strategy. The buy-and-hold strategy can be costly. One example of this is selling your winners and buying more of your losers to rebalance your portfolio back to its initial fixed weights, just before a big market recovery. Active money managers may be able to bring new capability to the table. Look for unique investment skills and be leery of too much personal attention by the sales force.

When advisors present complicated plans of how to invest your money, ask them to keep it simple. Evaluate simple ideas first, and consider complicated products last. Try to measure both cost and benefits. Try to determine the benefits both to your family and to the advisor. Does your advisor have an agenda? Do your homework and ask questions.

Ask if your advisors are fiduciaries who must put your interests ahead of theirs. Be wary of high commission products offered by non-fiduciaries. Ask about liquidity, commissions, and back-end surrender charges in case you change your mind.

How a Passive Trip-Advisor Can Ruin Your Journey

You are planning a 60-day trip from Miami to London in your 120-foot sailboat. You plan to leave September 1st. You have dreamed of this voyage your entire life. Your trip-advisor monitors the weather satellite forecasts before setting sail. You both check your sails, your supplies, your navigation equipment and communications. Your trip-advisor runs sail boat trajectory analysis by computer employing the latest Monte Carlo (random number scenario) analysis of all possible weather states, accounting for the last 20 years of data. Using these vast quantities of weather data your trip-advisor determines the best fixed-sail and fixed-rudder settings to get you safely to your London destination without any large course changes. And at the last minute your trip-advisor welds the sail and rudder in their fixed positions for you, and declines to go along with you. After all, your trip is not her dream journey. You are happy at first, having listened to your trip-advisor who fastened your sails and your rudder to their "average expected condition" positions. But, in spite of all your dreams and hopes for a calm ocean, just a few days into your journey, a hurricane forms unexpectedly off the West coast of Africa. After 50 days you begin to realize you have been blown way off course and you will eventually end up in the Arctic Circle with no provisions left. Why, you wonder, did you listen to that **trip-advisor** who assured you that you would achieve your goal with **fixed** sail and rudder positions?

This story is meant to illustrate that fixed passive asset allocation (buy-and-hold) might be disastrous. Especially if your allocation is based on 3, 5, or 30 years of historical data and your portfolio "sails" into a bear market. After all, a good portfolio for a bear market is different than for a bull market.

5. Classical and Tactical Asset Allocation Strategies

Investment Processes: Classical: buy-and-hold

A side-by-side comparison is given in Table 24 of the wealth management investment process for both classical and active (tactical) investment processes.

Table 24. Comparison of Classical and Tactical Investment Processes: Classical or Tactical.

Classical investment process, MPT optimization from wealth manager/planner without own track record, buys-and-hold

1. Investor questionnaire

- Goals, income
- Time horizon
- Risk tolerance
- Constraints, taxes.

2. Define asset allocation—MPT computer generated

- Initial and always allocation from MPT optimization with constraints
- 60/40 equity/bond typical
- 3 to 20 year statistics input
- Reallocation 1 to 4 times/year.

3. Implementation: manage other money managers and client expectation

- Hire money manager or buy mutual funds to manage a portion of portfolio
- Purchase hedge fund allocation from hedge fund manager
- Equity/bond constant typical 60/40
- Sell winners and buy losers to keep with original asset allocation.

4. Monitor/review

- Yearly to quarterly meeting with client
- Review portfolio allocation and return just before meeting
- Reallocate after meeting
- Hire/fire money managers, mutual fund managers, hedge fund managers
- Quarterly reports.

Tactical investment process with market timing from money manager with own track record

1. Investor questionnaire

- Goals, income
- Time horizon
- Risk tolerance
- Constraints, taxes.

2. Define asset allocation

- Initial allocation from optimization, 1/n weights, or estimate weights
- Determine % bonds needed from time horizon and risk profile
- Initial allocation from optimization, 1/n weights, or estimate weights
- Statistics less than 1 year.

3. Implementation: manage portfolio

- Continuous quantification of fund/ETF return/risk (daily, weekly); fund/ETF selection
- Measure fund/bond/ETF return and risk on a daily or weekly basis
- Reallocate often to stay in "best" funds/ETFs
- Employ optimization or 1/n weights
- Statistics less than 1 year
- Determine overall bull or bear market condition and cash/short positions
- Continuously buy/sell mutual funds, index funds, ETF, hedge funds
- Sell losers and buy winners.

4. Monitor/review

- Yearly to quarterly meeting with client
- Quarterly reports.

The wealth management investment process for a strategic asset allocation strategy is illustrated in Table 25. The process is described, and changes for tactical asset allocation are addressed later.

Table 25. Investment Process: Classical, buy-and-hold.

Classical investment process, MPT optimization from wealth manager/planner without own track record

1. Investor questionnaire

- Goals, income
- Time horizon
- Risk tolerance
- Constraints, taxes.

2. Define asset allocation—MPT computer generated

- Initial and always allocation from MPT optimization with constraints
- 60/40 equity/bond typical
- 3 to 20 year statistics input
- Reallocation 1-4 times/year.

3. Implementation: manage other money managers and client expectation

- Equity/bond constant typical 60/40
- Hire money manager and/or fund manager to manage a portion of portfolio
- Buy hedge fund allocation from hedge fund manager
- Sell winners and buy losers to keep with original asset allocation.

4. Monitor/review

- Yearly to quarterly meeting with client
- Review portfolio allocation and return just before meeting
- Reallocate after meeting

- Hire/fire money managers, mutual fund managers, hedge fund managers
- Quarterly reports.

Positives for WM with traditional buy-and-hold money management approach include:

- Little monitoring involved, end of quarter mostly (not day-to-day)
- High fee for little work, typically 1 to1.5 % fee
- A lot of the planner's work is to lower client expectations and to buy "average" portfolio

Problems with the buy-and-hold money management approach include:

- Market returns are never constant
- Current positions in the business cycle favors different sectors at different times
- When a fund is out of favor, it may be sold at the bottom
- Statistical historical inputs into the computer program optimizer are never correct because they are at best, long term averages are not useful in the short run
- Losing equity markets occur roughly 28% of the time.
- Gaining equity markets occur roughly 72% of the time.
- Buy-and-hold a static asset allocation process sells winners and buy losers
- Usually can't get average market returns.

Capital preservation in a down market is one notable strategy left out in buy-and-hold money management. Since very few mutual funds will take the mutual fund to cash or go short in a down market, the wealth manager who functions as investment advisor is responsible for capital preservation. **An investment plan without provisions to go short or to cash, in stressed markets, is not a plan!**

Bear Market Effect on Investing

Bear markets are usually defined when the S&P500 loses 20% or more from a peak. There were 13 bear markets from 1933 to 2007. Average losses are around 40% and average time to recover losses is about 3.5 years. If possible it is good to avoid these loses by market timing. Bear markets statistics are listed in Table 26.

Table 26. Bear Market Losses and Years to Recover.
(Source: *Meadors Investments,* < http://www.meadorsinvestments.com>).

Bear Markets—S&P 500 Index			
Bear Markets	Months	Loss	Years to Recover
07/33-03/35	20	33.9%	2.3
03/37-03/38	12	54.5%	8.8
11/38-04/42	22	45.8%	6.4
05/46-03/48	14	28.1%	4.1
08/56-11/57	14	21.6%	2.1
12/61-06/62	6	28.0%	1.8
02/66-10/66	8	22.2%	1.4
11/68-05/70	18	36.1%	3.3
01/73-10-74	21	48.2%	7.6
11/80-08/82	21	27.1%	2.1
08/87-12/87	4	33.5%	1.9
07/90-10/90	3	19.9%	0.6
09/00-03/03	30	49.0%	

From the bear market loss data one can see why it is a myth not to time the market. From earlier data than listed in Table 26, for an investor who bought-and-held in 1929 it took 25 years to get even. For the buy-and-hold investor who bought in 1973, it took 7.6 years to get even. Many advisors don't actively asset allocate or time the market because they can't. They hold to the buy-and-hold strategy to diversify, and not manage. Their plan is to over-diversify and periodically rebalance at client meetings.

Dynamic Asset Allocation

Dynamic asset allocation is also called tactical asset allocation and market timing. There are many different types of strategies. If in a bear market, capital preservation needs to be employed. A flow diagram is illustrated below in Table 27. The active allocation strategy is constantly monitored compared to only once or twice a year in a buy-and-hold approach.

Investment Processes: Tactical

Table 27. Investment Process: Tactical.

Tactical investment process with market timing from money manager with own track record

1. Investor questionnaire

- Goals, income
- Time horizon
- Risk tolerance
- Constraints, taxes.

2. Define asset allocation

- Initial allocation from optimization, 1/n weights, or estimate weights
- Determine % bonds needed from time horizon and risk profile
- Initial allocation from optimization, 1/n weights, or estimate weights
- Statistics less than 1 year.

3. Implementation: manage portfolio

- Continuous quantification of fund/ETF return/risk (daily, weekly); fund/ETF selection
- Measure fund/bond/ETF return and risk on a daily or weekly basis
- Reallocate often to stay in "best" funds/ETFs

- Employ optimization or 1/n weights
- Statistics less than 1 year
- Determine overall bull or bear market condition and cash/short positions
- Continuously buy/sell mutual funds, index funds, ETF, hedge funds
- Sell losers and buy winners,

4. Monitor/review

- Quarterly to yearly meeting with client
- Quarterly reports.

Historical Returns for Buy-and-Hold (Not Managed)

Many buy-and-hold advisors use long-term averages as targets for client portfolios in their unmanaged mutual fund program that are sold to clients. A 68 year-long compounded common stock return is 10.2 %. Using one standard deviation (68% of the time) would return, in any given year, between + 44.8% (10.2% + 34.6%) and -24.4% (10.2%-34.6%) return, see Table 28. This example illustrates that investors should not assume average return each and every year, because the investment process is not constant.

Table 28. Annual Returns 1926-1994.
(Source: Ibbotson, Annual Returns 1926-1994, 1995).

Asset class	compounded return, %	standard deviation, %
U.S. treasury bills	3.7%	3.3%
Intermediate Government bonds	5.1	5.7
Common stock	10.2	34.6
Inflation	3.1	4.6

Asset Class Performance Next Year is Not Last Year's Winner

Data showing eight domestic and international asset class performances from 1987 to 2006 are listed in Table 29. This shows that the best asset classes vary from one year to the next as the years move along.

Thus with a buy-and-hold approach, with a static domestic or foreign asset allocation, one would not participate in the best asset classes each year. In contrast to this, often investors buy last year's best fund or asset class only to see it drop later. And mutual fund managers try very hard to stay within their chosen universe and generally do not attempt to protect capital in down markets because by prospectus they are almost always long. With the advent of sector funds and ETFs it is practical to often and inexpensively reallocate to the best domestic sectors and/or country indexes. This can be a labor intensive and rewarding chore on a quasi-real time basis.

Dr. Gary J. Harloff, Ph.D

Table 29. Asset Class Index Performance Varies From Year-to-Year 1987-2006.
(Source: Callan, "Annual Returns for Key Indices (1987-2006), <http://www.callan.com/resource/>).

Annual Returns for Key Indices (1987–2006)
Ranked in order of performance (Best to Worst)

- S&P500 market weighted large cap index of 500 companies. Represents U.S. industry, not stock market.
- S&P500 Citi group growth and value.
- MSCI EAFE Morgan Stanley Capital International Europe, Australia, Far East.
- LB Aggregate Lehman Brothers bond index of U.S. government and corporate backed securities, 1 year or more maturity.

Harloff has analyzed the annual returns from the 8 indexes from 1987 to 2006. The data are from the Callan chart in Table 29. The average return vs. risk is illustrated in Figure 2 and shows Lehman Brothers aggregate bond index with the lowest return and risk. The equity returns are between 10 and 15% per year. The MSCI EAFE return is about 10% per year.

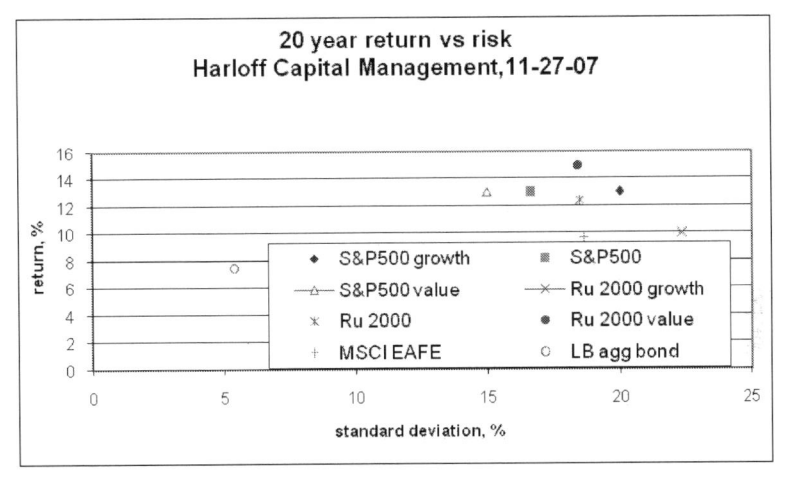

(Source: Harloff Capital Management).

Figure 2. 20 Year Return vs. Risk, 1987 to 2006 Yearly Asset Class Index Performance.

The average return and risk data from Figure 2 are also provided in Table 30.

Table 30. Average Return and Risk for Asset Class Indexes, 1987-2006.
(Source: Harloff Capital Management).

	Average return	Standard deviation, risk
MSCI EAFE	9.67 %	18.63 %
S&P500 growth	13.03	20.00
S&P500	13.03	16.62
S&P500 value	12.99	14.99
LB Agg	7.47	5.40
Ru2000 value	14.95	18.42
Ru2000	12.40	18.48
Ru2000 growth	10.03	22.32

Harloff conducted a timing study with data from 1986 to 2006, with benefit of hindsight. The asset class indexes is ranked from worst to best, in each year, and weighted such that the sum of the weights in each year is one. For each year, the worst return index is weighted 0. The equity curves for perfect timing and buy-and-hold for Ru 2000 and S&P500 are illustrated in Figure 3. The perfect timing portfolio holds up to 8 indexes in its portfolio. The perfect timing case indicates that $1. grows to $50.64 and the buy-and-hold Ru2000 grows to $12.52 and the buy-and-hold S&P500 grows to $9.31. This example provides a measure of timing potential over time. In this case timing is only done once a year because the return data are yearly. Much higher returns are possible, at least with hindsight, when asset allocation frequency increases. The annual compound rates of return are: timing 21.68%, Ru 2000 value 13.47%, and S&P500 11.80%. Notice that the compound rates of return differ from the algebraic average numbers listed in Table 30. Compounded and average rate of return are not the same. No expenses or fees are charged to any of the data. Generally no trading fees are incurred by trading fund indexes at the institutional level; a professional management fee, if managed, would lower the timing gain.

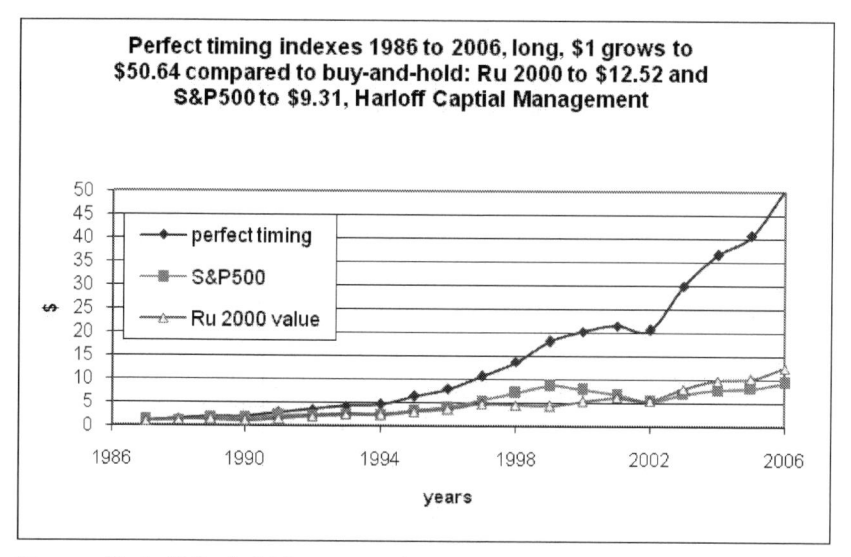

(Source: Harloff Capital Management).

Figure 3. Perfect Timing Index $1. Grows to $50.64 Compared to $12.52 RU 2000 Value Buy-and-Hold, 1986-2006. Hypothetical No Fees.

The perfect asset allocation timing weights are illustrated in Figure 4. The largest weight is the sum of all the equity index funds. Equity weight varies from 50 to 100% depending on the year. The bond weight varies from 0 to 40%, and the EAFE weight varies from 0 to 38%. These weights are clearly not constant and large variations from year to year are computed.

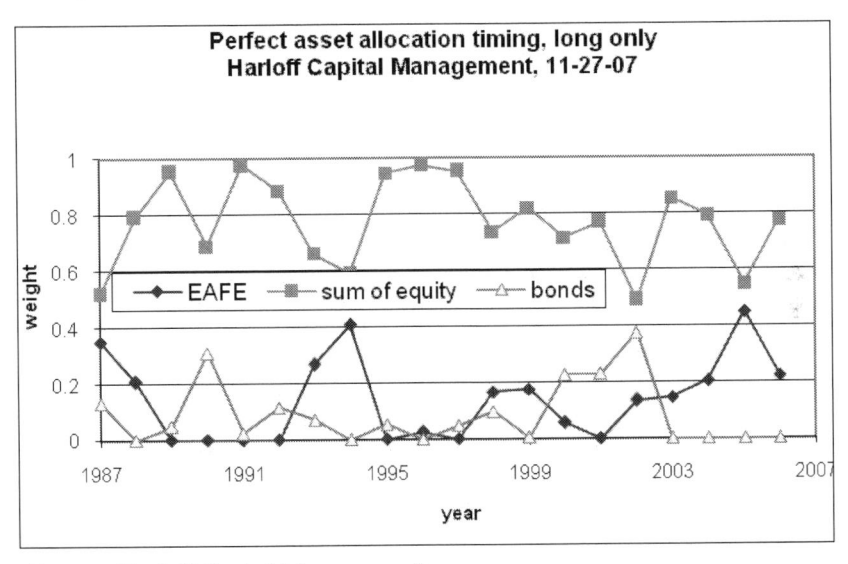

(Source: Harloff Capital Management).

Figure 4. Asset Allocation Weights for Optimal Timing Indexes, 1987-2007.

Dr. Gary J. Harloff, Ph.D

6. Math of Investing

(adapted from: Amit Goyal, HEC Lausanne, MS of Science in Finance, Investments, Fall 2007, <https://www.hec.unil.ch/docs/agoyal/cours/16>)

Total Return

Total return, r_{t+1}, is the gain including dividends from one time period to another divided by the initial investment, i.e.:

$$r_{t+1} = \{[P_{t+1} + D_{t+1}]\}/P_t - 1$$

Where
r_{t+1} = total return
P_t = price today, t
P_{t+1} = price tomorrow, t+1
D_{t+1} = dividend received tomorrow, t+1

Return over multiple periods is the product of the returns for each individual time. As an example over two periods, R_{t+2}, consider two products, i.e.

$$(1+ R_{t+2}) = (1+ r_{t+1})(1+ r_{t+2})$$

R_{t+2} = return from t to t+2
r_{t+1} = return from time t to t+1
r_{t+2} = return from time t+1 to t+2

Compound Return

Compound return is the total return over the total time period examined. For example, suppose the return in year 1 is 10 % and in year 2 is 20 %. The compound return is:

$(1+ 0.1)(1+ 0.2) - 1 = 0.32$ or 32%

Compound return is not the sum of returns.

Using the same 10% and 20% example above, the average annual compound return, <r>, over two years is:

$$(1+ <r>)(1+ <r>) = (1+ r_1)(1+ r_2)$$

Finding the average compound return, <r>:

$$<r> = \sqrt{\{(1+r_1)(1+r_2)\}} - 1 = \sqrt{\{(1.1)(1.2)\}} - 1 = .149 = 14.9\%$$

As a check, see if $<r> = 0.32 = (1+ 0.149)^2 - 1$. This checks here.

Inflation

Computing inflation adjusted return (real return) is useful because it removes the inflation effect (with a divisor) as illustrated below. As a rule of thumb, U.S. government bonds return about the inflation rate. Thus investing in bonds essentially keeps one's real money even (no growth and no loss) after inflation.

i = inflation rate

$$1+ r_{real} = (1 + r_{nominal})/(1 + i)$$

$$r_{real} = (1 + r_{nominal})/(1 + i) - 1$$

As an example, consider a nominal return, $r_{nominal}$, of = 12%, with inflation, i = 3%

$$r_{real} = (1+ 0.12)/(1+ 0.03) - 1$$

$$r_{real} = 8.74\%$$

Thus the inflation adjusted return is 8.74%. Inflation is not simply subtracted from the return.

Foreign Investment and Currency Effect on Annual Returns

In the past several years the U.S. dollar has inflated compared to many other currencies like the Euro and many investors sought higher return overseas. Consider an example with a return of 21.% in Euro land when the cost of one Euro on 9/30/2006 was $1.28 and one year later the cost of one Euro increased to $1.47. The Euro appreciated in terms of the U.S. dollar. The return corrected for currency is:

Return US = [currency end value in US/currency begin value in US] x return.

Thus if the return in Euros was 21% then the return in US is:

Return US = {1.47/1.28 }[1.21] = 1.148 x 1.21 = 1.39 or 39% after adjusting for the currency difference. When the US dollar goes down relative to another growing country, some money will flow to the other country to earn higher dollar adjusted returns.

Risk

危機 is the Chinese symbol for risk. It is a combination of a first symbol for danger and a second symbol for opportunity. Both return and risk should be managed and quantified to the extent possible.

Risks include loss of capital, inflation, loss of investment opportunity, volatility of return, etc. Financial services usually quantify investment risk as standard deviation, a mathematical measure of root mean square (average) of the absolute difference from the mean, over a time period.

Portfolio Optimization

Markowitz invented "Modern" portfolio theory (MPT) in his 1953 Ph.D. (graduation date is 1955) thesis from the University of Chicago and his math model is still used today. He developed a math procedure to quantify optimal portfolio asset allocation returns for various risk levels. The rudiments of portfolio optimization are discussed below. He won the Nobel Prize in Economics in 1990.

Markowitz used expected or average return and risk for each stock, variance (σ^2_x or standard deviation squared) for each stock, and covariance of returns for each stock. Sharpe, who also won the Nobel Prize in Economics in 1990, reformulated and simplified the Markowitz model to be relative to a reference investment or index, usually taken to be the S&P500. (A good reference is Sharpe, W. F. "Portfolio Theory and Capital Markets", 1970, McGraw-Hill.)

Simplified Sharpe Approach
Return = alpha + beta (Return $_{reference}$)

In simple terms, the math model optimizer solves for portfolio allocation weights, w_i, from 0 to 1 (long only), of the best stocks to invest in. Inputs to the model include: expected mean return, expected variation of return, and return correlations, for each stock considered.

For a two stock portfolio, the portfolio weights are:

w_x and w_y, and their sum, $w_x + w_y$, adds up to 1.0.

The expected (mean) return for each of the two stocks are: μ_x and μ_y

The portfolio mean return is the sum of the individual weighted mean returns:

$\mu_p = w_x \mu_x + w_y \mu_y$

The expected or historical variance of return, or σ^2, for each stock, are: σ^2_x and σ^2_y

and using the notation i for either x or y and using the notation E for expected value:

$\sigma^2_i = E[r_i - E(r_i)]^2$

or

$\sigma^2_i = E\{r_i - E(r_i)][r_i - E(r_i)]\}$

The interaction term is the product risk of the (two) stocks. It quantifies the effect of each risk on the portfolio risk through a risk product term. This term is called covariance, and is noted as σ_{xy}:

$$\sigma_{xy} = \rho_{xy} \sigma_x \sigma_y$$

where correlation coefficient, ρ_{xy} is a number between +1 and -1. This number "explains" how the variation of one parameter corresponds to the variation of another parameter.

The portfolio variance, σ_p^2, is the weighted sum of individual asset variances plus a cross risk term of the covariance weighted by the portfolio weights, i.e.

$$\sigma_p^2 = w_x^2 \sigma_x^2 + w_y^2 \sigma_y^2 + 2 w_x w_y \sigma_{xy}$$

The third term above with covariance, σ_{xy}, is important as it increases or decreases the portfolio risk depending on its sign. This term leads to a curved or nonlinear relationship between optimal return and risk as illustrated below.

Example of Portfolio Optimization

Using a portfolio optimizer computer program, assumed inputs, and constraints (if any), optimized returns can be obtained for different levels of risk. The result of the optimization is a curved optimal line usually called the "efficient frontier"; see Figure 5. Generally John Doe's current portfolio can be shown to lie below the line and shows that his portfolio is not "optimal". Note the dates employed in defining the statistical inputs are from May 1997 to August 2005, and cover 8.5 years. Thus the expected average yearly return should be between 4.5% and 10.5% if one buys and holds and the economy doesn't tank. Of course the stock market's character is assumed to be the same as the past 8.5 years character.

Some WM or financial planners understand the assumptions, math, data limitations, and the nuances of the portfolio optimizer computer programs. However, few have actually designed and programmed the optimizers. Without an adequate understanding of optimization limitations, a WM might actually harm an individual's investment portfolio.

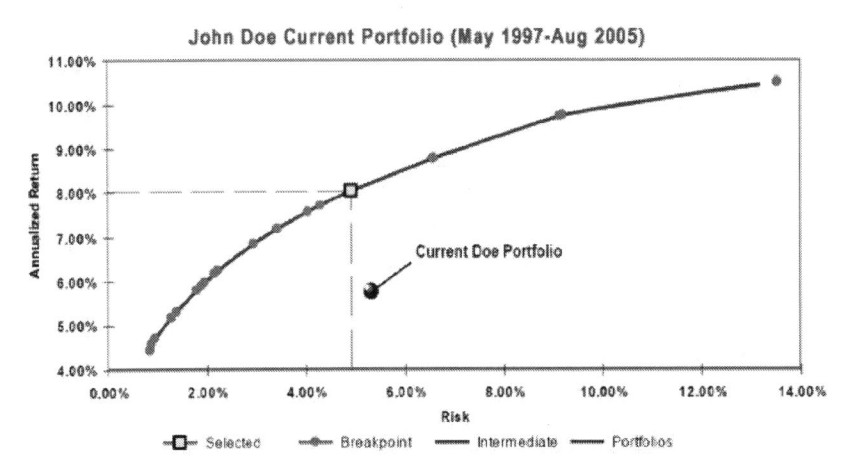

John Doe Current Portfolio (May 1997-Aug 2005)

(Source: Partnervest Financial Group LLC, <http://www.partnervest.com/Investment-Management-Services.html>).

Figure 5. Return and Risk Efficient Frontier.

This ends the theory part of modern portfolio theory. The important points are that the return and risk numbers for each asset considered must be assumed because future returns and statistics are not available. A really big part of this theory is the implicit assumption that the input numbers are assumed to be constant numbers. In reality, none of these input numbers are constants unless they are averaged over 3, 5, or 30 years. If a bear market is encountered many investors will probably abandon their MPT portfolio allocations with the conclusion that the theory doesn't work. This is discussed further below.

Problems with Modern Portfolio Theory in 2000 Bear Market

During the late 1990's and early 2000's the Nasdaq technology market inflated over the S&P500 index as illustrated below in Figure 6. This price inflation was partly caused by the government's spending on the year 2000 Cobal programming projects to fix the perceived millennium date problems in financial computer programs and on related business spending on technology. Early in 2000 the Federal Open Market Committee, FOMC, reduced the money supply and equity speculation declined due to a reduced margin capability. A severe and historic bear market followed and the Nasdaq 100 index has yet to recover from the year 2000 levels.

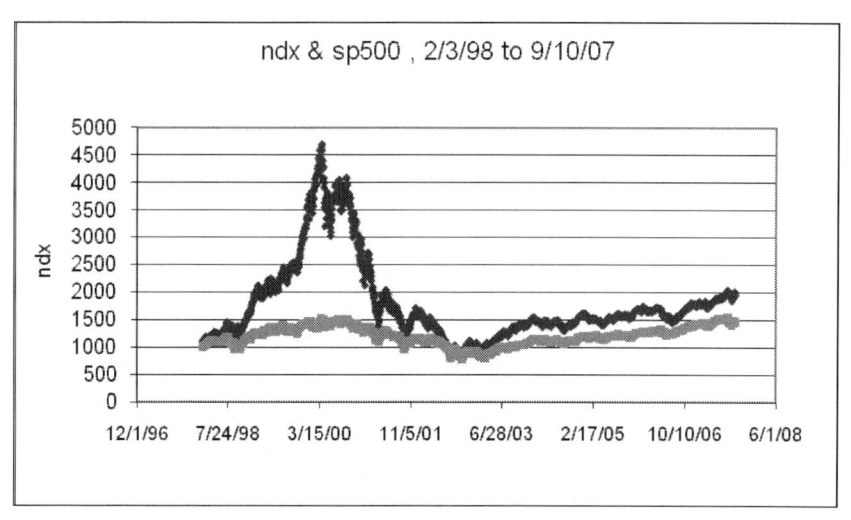

[Figure: ndx & sp500, 2/3/98 to 9/10/07]

(Source: Harloff Capital Management 9/2007).

Figure 6. Nasdaq 100 (Higher Line) and S&P500 (Lower Line) Prices From 2/3/1998 to 9/10/2007.

Trading Strategies

There are trading strategies that attempt to take advantage of large up and/or down market movements by being long when the market goes up and short, or in cash, when the market goes down. There are few trading strategies that work on both the S&P500 and the Nasdaq 100 indexes; the strategy illustrated below is one system that works on both indexes. As a reference $1.00 originally in the S&P500 index grows to $1.51 in a buy-and-hold approach from 2-2-98 to 9-10-07. By market timing the same $1. grows to $5.25, as illustrated in Figure 7. Notice that there are periods of rapid gain and other periods where the gains are less dramatic with small ups and downs. Since we live in a "now" culture, it is possible for an investor to conclude that a sound trading system, with recent lackluster returns, no longer works just when gains are on the horizon.

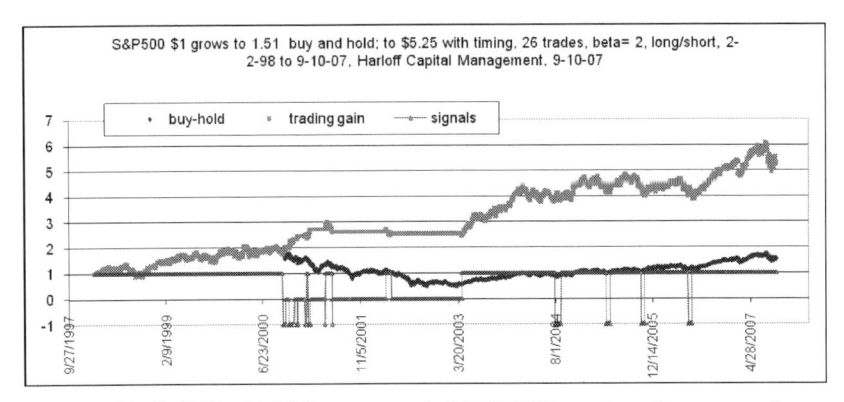

(Source: Harloff Capital Management, 9/10/2007, past performance does not insure future performance).

Figure 7. Trading Strategy (Hypothetical) Showing $1.00 Growing to $5.25 for S&P500 Whereas Buy-and-Hold Grows to $1.51 from 2/2/1998 to 9/10/2007.

The same computer program and trading logic produces good results with the more volatile NDX index. For the NDX index with timing, $1.00 grows to $41.11 from 2/2/1998 to 9/10/2007 where as the buy-and-hold approach drops to $0.93, see Figure 8. The long and short signals (+1 and -1 respectively) are included in the graph. It is unusual for one trading strategy to provide good results on different indexes due to different volatility and time histories.

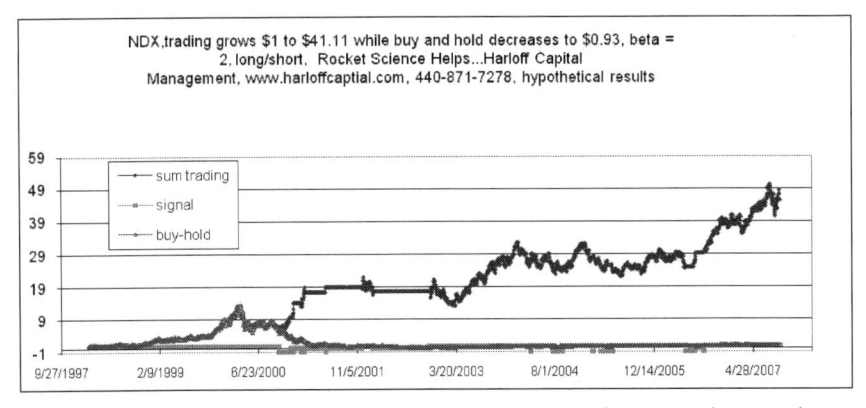

(Source: Harloff Capital Management, 9/10/2007, past performance does not insure future performance).

Figure 8. Trading Strategy (Hypothetical) Showing $1.00 Growing to $41.11 for NDX Whereas Buy-and-Hold Drops to $0.93 from 2/2/1998 to 9/10/2007.

Absolute and Relative Investing and Alpha and Beta

In the alternate investment area of hedge funds, there is much discussion on alpha and beta. These variables are always relative to a reference investment or index. The following examples relate the Nasdaq 100 (NDX) performance to the S&P500 reference index performance. Alpha is defined to be the return of the NDX when the return of the S&P500 is zero, i.e. the intercept of the graph below. And beta is defined to be the relative gain of the NDX compared to the S&P500 gain, i.e. the slope of the curve below.

Today, much of investing is based on relative performance. In Figure 9 the average daily NDX change is 1.6354 times the average daily change of the S&P500 index. This is beta and is simply the slope of the line. The NDX change at zero S&P500 change, i.e. the intercept, is 0.0001. Although not widely appreciated in the planner financial industry, both alpha and beta are dependent on the time interval selected as illustrated below.

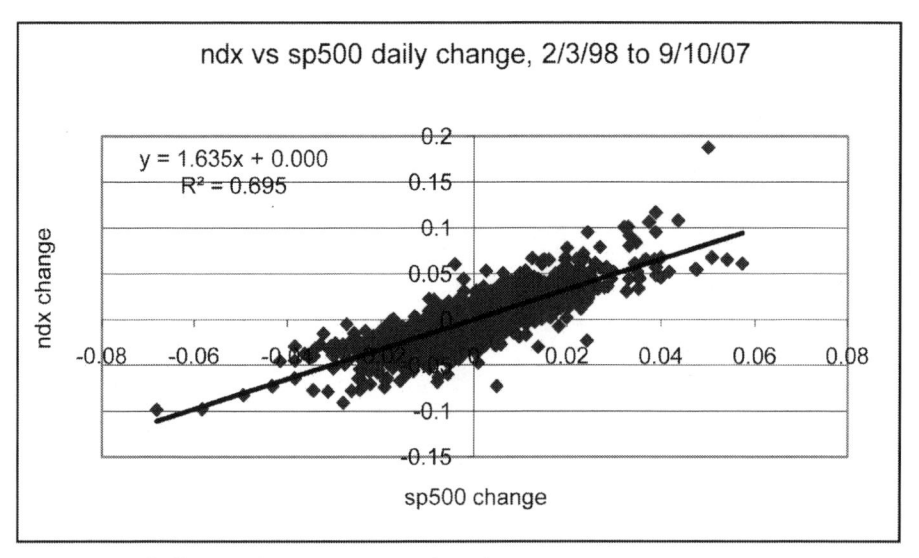

(Source: Harloff Capital Management 9/2007).

Figure 9. Nasdaq 100, NDX, Change vs. S&P500 Change Daily From 2/3/1998 to 9/10/2007.

To compute alpha per year a few other statistics are needed. The standard deviation of NDX = 0.022, i.e. the average daily change is 2.2%. Investors who buy and sell within the daily average change of 2.2% are sometimes called "noise" traders. The standard deviation of S&P500 is 0.011331, where the average daily change is 1.13%. (It is interesting that the daily average percentage change of 2.2% and 1.13%, for the NDX and S&P500 respectively, are similar to yearly money management fees). These values describe how "volatile" or different the daily prices are from the average price change. The ratio of the standard deviations is 1.9612 = 2.2/1.13. The correlation coefficient squared describes how well the equation fits (or explains) the data, and from the graph we read that R^2 is 0.6953. The square root of R^2 is 0.8338.

We compute beta by multiplying the ratio of the standard deviations by R, i.e. beta = 1.9612 * 0.8338 = 1.63.

We compute alpha by computing a yearly return based on the intercept = $(0.00013+1)^{252} - 1$ = 0.0328, i.e. the NDX would return 3.28% in an average year when the S&P500 returns zero. We have used 252 "market open" days per year.

Another way to compute alpha it is to use the intercept function in an XCEL spreadsheet or XLS code, i.e. alpha =(intercept (cn1:cn2,bn1:bn2)+1)^{252}-1.

It is instructive to compute and compare the values of alpha and beta of the NDX index relative to the S&P500 index over the entire period to the values over both the bull period and the bear period, see Table 31. Some advisors might incorrectly say that these alpha and beta values are constant and not variable over any period, possibly because of receiving little training in statistical data analysis and interpretation. This is where an Engineering degree is helpful.

An inflation bubble of a bull run, from 12-31-1998 to 12-31-1999, is clearly indicated by the alpha (or intercept) increasing dramatically from an average value of 3.28% to 60.35 % per year. In a similar manner, the bear market alpha from 3-24-2000 to 10-9-2002, is -7.7% per year and is also very different from the average alpha value of 3.28%. The beta or slope value is not very different over the time periods analyzed, because the ratio of the standard deviations is not much different.

Table 31. Variation of Alpha and Beta of NDX vs. S&P500 for Three Time Periods.
(Source: Harloff Capital Management, 9/2007).

Time period	Dates	Alpha, % per year	Beta relative to S&P500	Standard deviation of NDX daily % change	Standard deviation of S&P500 daily % change
Several years	2-3-98 to 9-10-07	3.28	1.64	2.22	1.13
Bull	12-31-98 to 12-31-99	60.35	1.55	2.10	1.14
Bear	3-24-00 to 10-9-02	-7.70	1.96	3.37	1.44

Very few investment sales professionals know how to compute alpha and beta, and few will appreciate how these quantities change with time. This is one way to quickly differentiate a salesperson from a money manager.

The graphical presentation of the bull and bear markets are shown in Figure 10 and Figure 11 respectively.

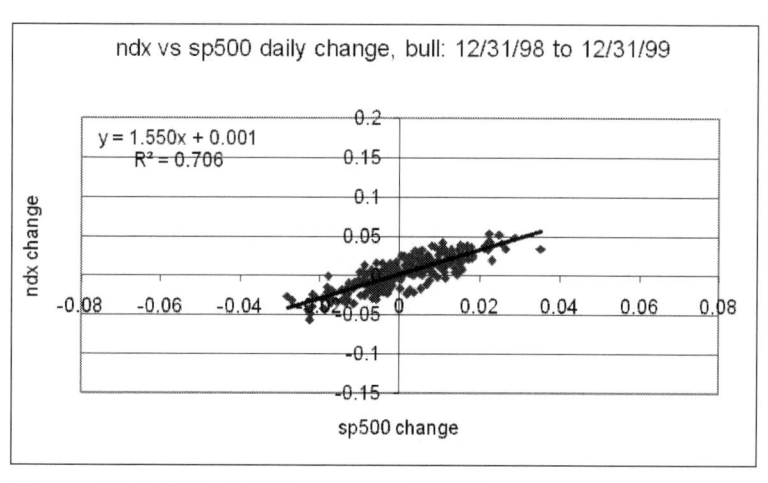

(Source: Harloff Capital Management 9/2007).

Figure 10. Daily Change of NDX vs. S&P500 During Bull Market From 12/31/1998 to 12/31/1998.

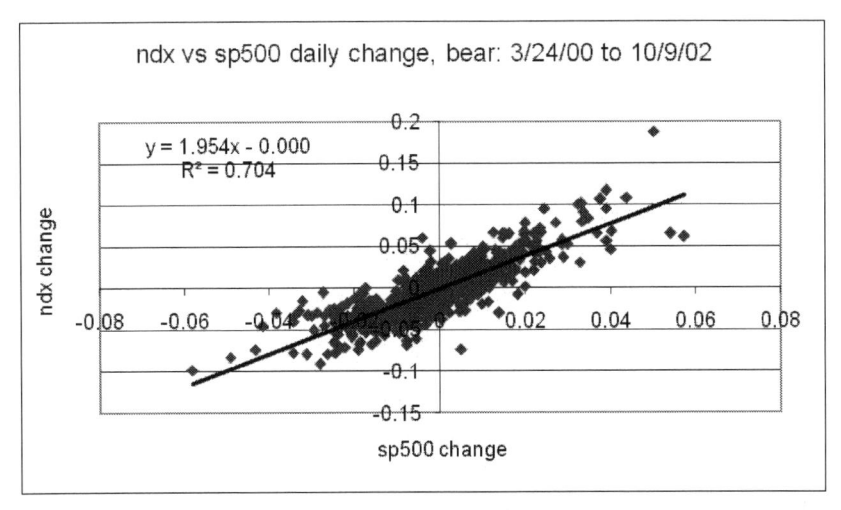

[Chart: ndx vs sp500 daily change, bear: 3/24/00 to 10/9/02; y = 1.954x - 0.000, $R^2 = 0.704$]

(Source: Harloff Capital Management 9/2007).

Figure 11. Daily Change of NDX vs. S&P500 During Bull market from 3/24/2000 to 10/9/2002.

Example of a Dynamic Asset Allocation Strategy

One way to profit by the changes in market and market sector direction is to change asset allocation with market changes. A 1998 hypothetical study by Harloff illustrates how investment pairs within asset classes can be alternately selected and how this strategy performance exceeds the buy-and-hold non-strategy. This dynamic asset allocation (DAA) strategy is to invest in the stronger of the two paired asset classes, for example: invest in either emerging market or money market, or in short-term bonds or aggressive growth. Asset classes are selected that have low correlations to each other. These paired primary and alternate asset pairs are listed in Table 32.

Over the 8 year study period the DAA strategy with 13 paired asset classes, increases buy-hold return by 330 basis points (bps) or 3.3% per year (from 12.7%/year to 16% per year). This is a 26% increase. Further, the DAA strategy increased the Sharpe ratio from 0.62 to 0.91 for a 47% increase. The utility of DAA is illustrated in Figure 12. This 1998 published study also introduces the concept of the "Dynamic Frontier", the time-varying efficient frontier. (Source: Harloff, G. J., "Dynamic Asset Allocation; Beyond Buy-and-Hold", Technical Analysis of Stocks and Commodities Magazine, January 1998).

Table 32. Dynamic Frontier Primary and Alternate Asset Class Pairs for a Preferred Dynamic Asset Allocation Strategy.
(Source: Harloff, G.J., "Dynamic Asset Allocation: Beyond Buy-and-Hold, Stocks and Commodities, January 1998).

DYNAMIC FRONTIER PRIMARY AND ALTERNATE ASSET CLASS PAIRS FOR PREFERRED DAA STRATEGY

Primary Asset Class	Alternate Asset Class for Preferred DAA	Correlation Coefficient	Rate of Return per Year, Percent	Sharpe Ratio	MDD
Precious Metals	Aggressive Growth	-0.03	14.7	0.50	28.0
OTC	International Equity	0.35	19.6	0.93	19.9
Aggressive	International Equity	0.36	21.7	1.07	19.9
Emerging Market	Money Market	0.05	19.0	1.09	11.2
Zero-Coupon Bond	Aggressive Growth	0.34	17.4	0.88	18.6
Fid Select	Long-Term Bond	0.40	14.7	0.92	10.8
Growth	International Equity	0.38	16.3	0.87	19.9
International Equity	Aggressive Growth	0.36	21.7	1.07	19.9
SP500 w/Div	International Equity	0.29	16.7	0.95	19.9
Growth-Inc	Money Market	0.08	11.1	0.96	4.8
Income	Money Market	0.11	10.9	1.05	4.2
Long-Term Bond	Money Market	0.33	8.9	0.81	3.9
Short-Term Bond	Aggressive Growth	0.24	15.7	0.77	10.5

Assuming equal asset class weighting, average rate of return = 16 percent and average Sharpe ratio = 0.91.

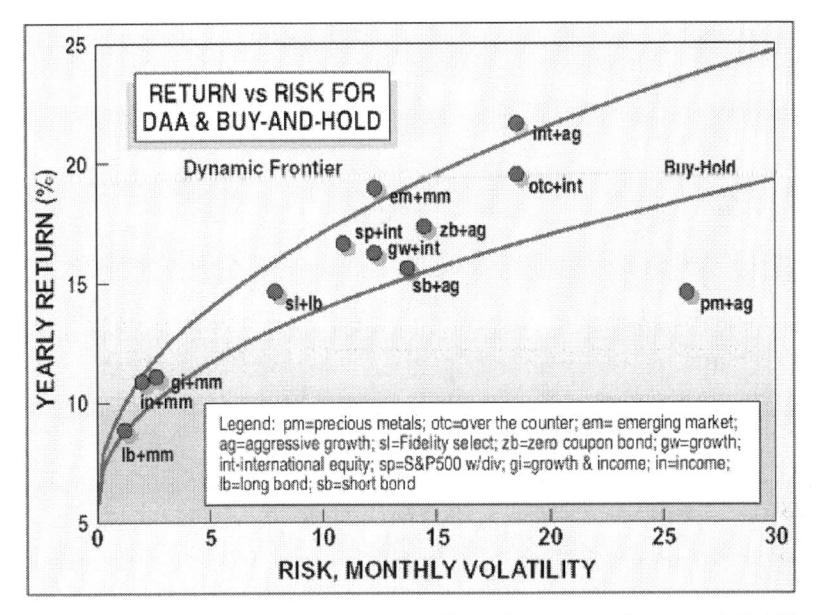

[Figure: Return vs Risk for DAA & Buy-and-Hold scatter plot]

(Source: Harloff, G.J., "Dynamic Asset Allocation: Beyond Buy-and-Hold", Technical Analysis of Stocks and Commodities Magazine, January 1998).

Figure 12. Yearly Return vs. Monthly Volatility or Risk.

Market Timing: the Best and Worst 10 days Over About 23 years

A common issue in market timing, raised by the buy-and-hold advocates, is that if one misses a few of the best days the yearly % return drops off a lot. Consider if an investor misses the best 10 days of the S&P500 index from 1/1/1980 to 12/21/2002. The return would have dropped from the buy-and-hold return of 9.55% to 7.03%. But missing both the best and worst 10 days increases the average return to 10.83% per year; see Table 33. Thus timing doesn't have to be perfect to provide value over buy-and-hold.

Table 33. Dynamic Asset Allocation Doesn't have to be Perfect to Beat Buy-and-Hold for S&P500 from 1/1/1980 to 12/31/2002.
(Source: Tandem Financial Services, Inc. Study, 2003).

	% per year
Buy-and-Hold	9.55
Missed 10 best days	7.03
Missed 20 best days	5.18
Missed 30 best days	3.57
Missed 40 best days	2.12
Missed 10 worst days	13.44
Missed 20 worst days	15.47
Missed 30 worst days	17.18
Missed 40 worst days	18.75
Missed 10 best & worst days	10.83
Missed 20 best & worst days	10.87
Missed 30 best & worst days	10.78
Missed 40 best & worst days	10.68

Expected Returns

It is an obvious myth that is rarely accomplished, that any portfolio can be designed to provide a certain % return per year. Most financial planners purchase very long-term statistics to compute optimal portfolio allocations. This is in spite of the fact that, as shown here, alpha, beta, variances, and correlation coefficients all vary with time and are not constants. Investors painfully experienced the limitations of assumed constant optimizer inputs and resulting fixed portfolios during the recent bear market from 2000 to 2003. It is common for planners and brokers to try to convince clients to hold their "optimal" asset allocation and sell winners to buy losers. This process may drive client portfolios deeper into the red for years. Some investors, planners, and brokers have since realized that buy-and-hold MPT doesn't work.

In a similar way that equity buy-and-hold portfolios don't deliver expected constant returns, income portfolios also provide uncertain returns.

Income Portfolio Example

Consider Ms. Smith, who needs to generate 4.8% cash flow each year. Typical money market, bond, and stock long-term investment returns are listed in Table 34:

Table 34. Income Portfolio Example for Ms. Smith.

Investment	interest	dividends	capital gains	total return
Money market	4%	0%	0%	4%
Bonds	6	0	0	6
Stock	0	2	9	11

Ms. Smith needs no cash reserve. Several bond allocations of 100, 70 and 50% would provide her with 6, 4.8, and 4.0%, respectively, cash flow as illustrated in Table 35. (A 2% dividend from stock is assumed). If her cash flow is generated from both dividends and interest, her minimum bond allocation is 70%, because a lower bond allocation will provide less than her 4.8% requirement, see Table 35. Many wealth managers might allocate a standard 60/40 (equity/bond ratio) instead. This example ignores capital gain from equities.

Table 35. Several Bond and Stock Allocations for Ms. Smith.

Bond Allocation	bonds cash flow	stock allocation	stock cash flow	total cash flow
100%	6.0	0%	0%	6.%
70	4.2	30	0.6	4.8
50	3.0	50	1.0	4.0

The tension between dividend return and real return is illustrated in see Table 36. A 100% stock allocation has an estimated portfolio total return (dividend return plus portfolio appreciation) of 11. %, and a 100% bond portfolio has a total return of 7.3%. These two different allocations have a sustainable withdrawal rate of 7.0% for 100% equities and 3.3% for

100% bonds, respectively, assuming the guessed average returns are real. Obviously the higher returning stock portfolio is predicted to last longer.

These examples assume perfect forecasting that is, unfortunately, not possible.

Table 36. Tension Between Yield and Appreciation.
(Source: Gibson, R. 1992 IAFP Advanced Planner Conference, 1992).

Vanguard bond allocation	100%	50%	0%
Vanguard index trust 500 allocation	0	50	100
Portfolio dividend return	7.3	5.1	2.9
Portfolio appreciation	*0*	*4.0*	*8.1*
Portfolio total return	7.3	9.1	11.0
Inflation	4.0	4.0	4.0
Sustainable real withdrawal rate	3.3	5.1	7.0

Tax Deferred Growth with a Variable or Fixed Annuity

There are many variable annuities with tax deferral for non-qualified (after tax) money. Some insurance contracts employ aggressive leveraged index long and short mutual funds. There are also fixed return index annuities. One example that beats CD rates is illustrated in see Figure 13. This generic product allows for an upside return of 8.5% and no downside losses. The surrender charge, of roughly 1% per year, should be considered in case you change your mind.

HYPOTHETICAL ANNUAL RESET

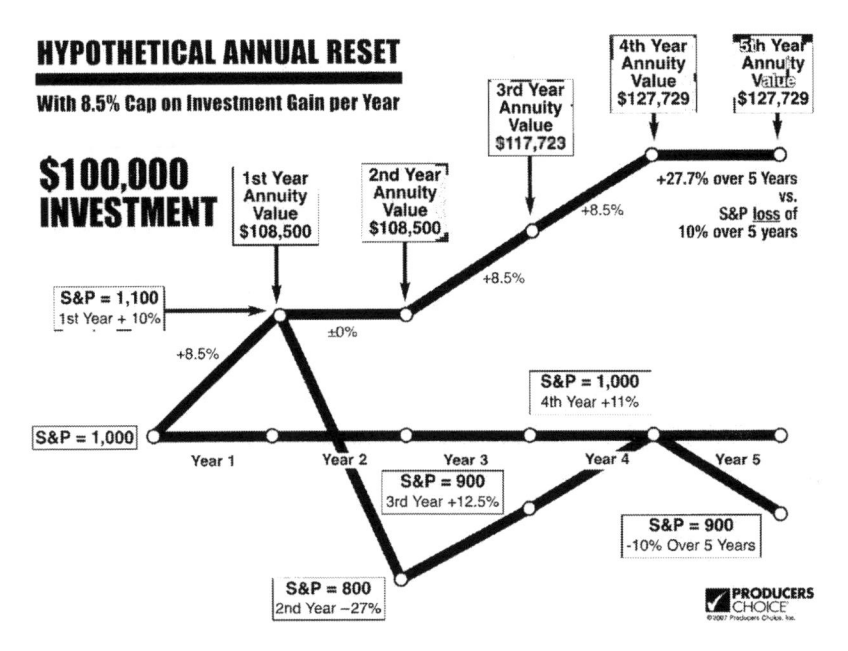

With 8.5% Cap on Investment Gain per Year

(Source: Producers Choice Generic Equity Index, Nov. 2007. Upside Limits and Guarantees Vary with Specific Index Annuity Contracts).

Figure 13. Example of Index Annuity.

Example Return Variation Over Time

An example of the variation of compounded annual returns is illustrated in Figure 14. This hypothetical return graph shows that the compounded returns can vary between 4 to 15% with risk levels between 15 to 30%.

EXHIBIT 4
FIFTEEN-YEAR ANNUAL COMPOUNDED RETURN AND RISK FOR THE PERIOD ENDING JUNE 30, 1993

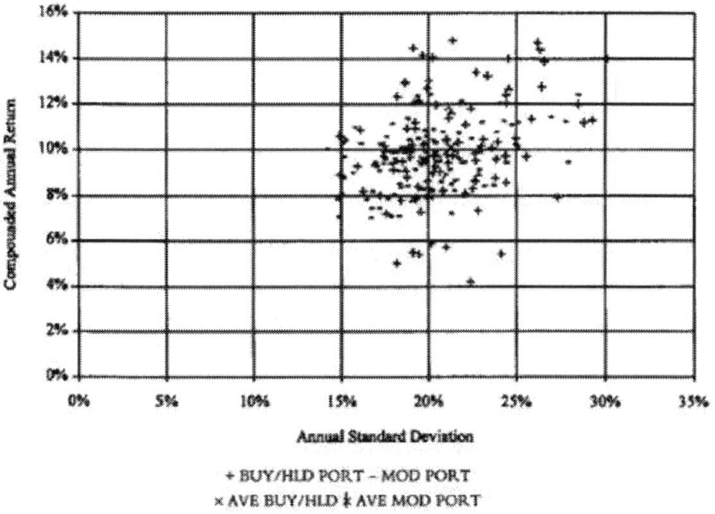
Compounded Annual Return
16%
14%
12%
10%
8%
6%
4%
2%
0%
0%
5%
10%
15%
20%
25%
30%
35%
Annual Standard Deviation
+ BUY/HLD PORT - MOD PORT
× AVE BUY/HLD ǂ AVE MOD PORT

SUMMER 1995

(Source: Applebach,R.O., Jr., “The Capital Gains Tax Penalty”, Journal of Portfolio Management, 1995).

Figure 14. Fifteen-Year Annual Compounded Return and Risk, Ending 6/30/1993.

7. Portfolio Theory Examples

There are many possible portfolio average return and average risk points, depending on how the stock allocation weights are selected and which stocks are included. Figure 15 shows some of the possible portfolio returns vs. risk with 5 stocks: MSFT, KO, GM, JPM, and ABUD, from 2000 to 2004. (Source: Goyal, A., "Course Notes", HEC Lausanne: Master of Science in Finance, Investments, Fall 2007, <https://www.hec.unil.ch/docs/agoyal/04.portfolio_optimization[1].ppt>)

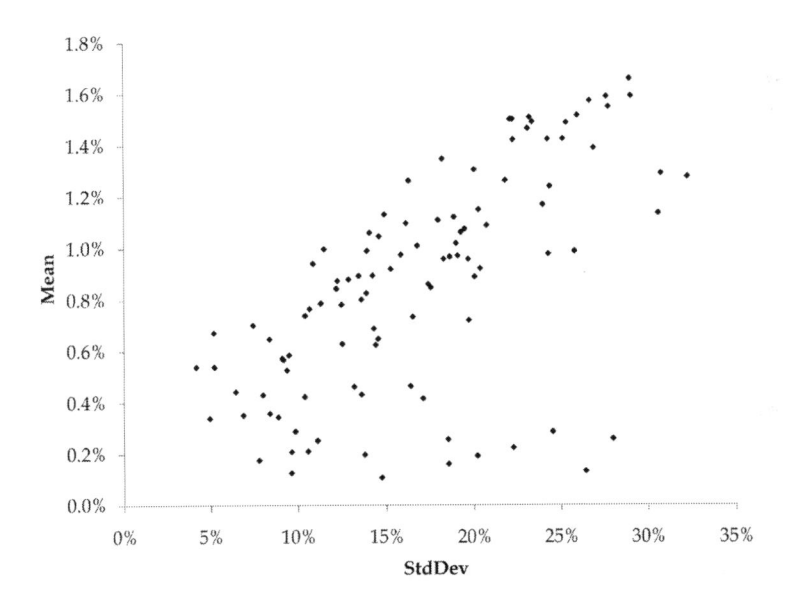

(Source: Source: Goyal, A., "Course Notes", HEC Lausanne: Master of Science in Finance, Investments, Fall 2007, <https://www.hec.unil.ch/docs/agoyal/cours/16>).

Figure 15. Sample Portfolio Mean Monthly Return and Standard Deviation.

Using the same 5 stocks and statistical data, an optimal set of return vs. risk can be obtained with an MPT calculation. The optimal return for a specified risk is called the optimized portfolio and is said to lie on the efficient frontier, see Figure 16. The Efficient Frontier line has the highest return for a given standard deviation or risk.

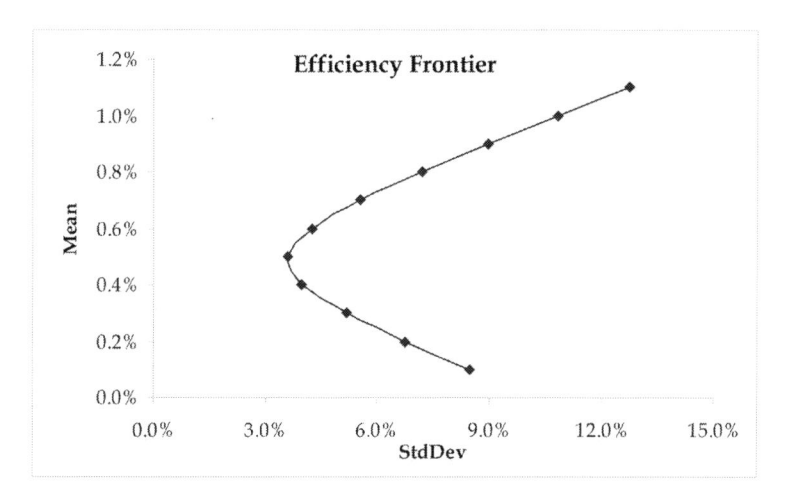

[Figure: Efficiency Frontier plot, Mean vs StdDev]

(Source: Source: Goyal, A., "Course Notes", HEC Lausanne: Master of Science in Finance, Investments, Fall 2007, <https://www.hec.unil.ch/docs/agoyal/cours/16>).

Figure 16. Optimized Portfolios Along Efficient Frontier, Mean and Monthly Standard Deviation.

Assumptions in the calculated procedure include:

- Statistical mean returns and variances (typically averaged over 3 to 20 years) are assumed constant
- The financial character of whole industries and companies are assumed stable over 3 to 20 years
- Correlation coefficients are assumed constant. (In reality these coefficients can vary widely with time. For example, international correlation coefficients can vary between + 1 and -1 over a few year period).

A tangent line from the risk free (T bill) return to the highest tangent to the "efficient" frontier, divided by the risk (or standard deviation) at that tangent point is the highest "Sharpe Ratio" (SR) defined as:

$$SR = (return - risk\ free\ return)/risk$$

This ratio is commonly used to compare return and risk, and is named after Professor Bill Sharpe. This ratio is not constant and changes most during large market moves and bear markets.

An example of two-asset class optimization to "forecast" a 12-month return and risk curve, employing 54 years of statistical data is illustrated in Figure 17. Notice that the large capitalization style is the low return result with 12% return and 16% risk. The high return point is small cap with 12.8% return and 23% risk.

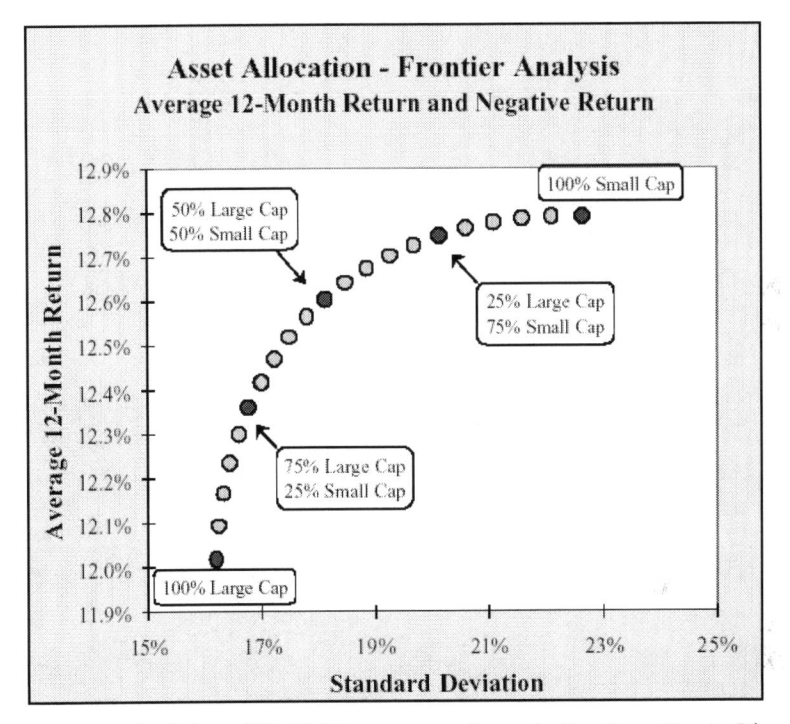

Asset Allocation - Frontier Analysis
Average 12-Month Return and Negative Return

(Source: Glenmede, Private Wealth Management Summit, San Juan Puerto Rico, April 18-20, 2002).

Figure 17. Efficient Frontier for S&P500 and Russell 2000 From 1946 to 2000.

A comparison of a client asset mix with a more diversified asset mix is typically shown to potential clients to demonstrate an increase in expected portfolio return and lower risk obtained by portfolio optimization. Additional asset classes are brought into the proposed new portfolio including: international, emerging market, private equity, and real estate.

A typical client presentation graphic is shown in Table 37. The idea is to show how an advisor can add value to an existing client portfolio. Note: standard deviations are based on historical data from 1970 to 2001.

Table 37. Typical Client Presentation Graphic.
(Source: Glenmede, Private Wealth Management Summit, San Juan Puerto Rico, April 18-20, 2002).

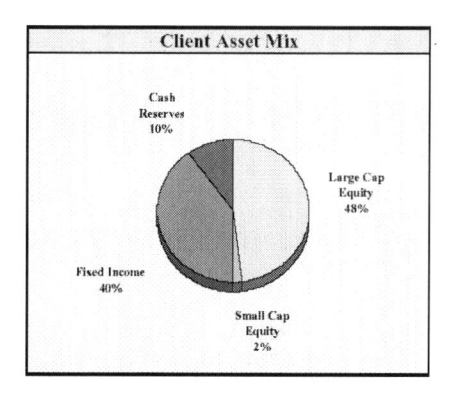

a) Client Asset Mix

Pie chart:
- Large Cap Equity 48%
- Fixed Income 40%
- Cash Reserves 10%
- Small Cap Equity 2%

Asset Composition
Stocks	50%
Fixed Income	40%
Cash	10%
Other	0%

Return/Risk
Expected Return	6.6%
Expected Income	2.7%
Standard Deviation	9.0%
Negative Return Frequency:	
12-Month Period	23.0%
60-Month Period	5.0%

b) Diversified Asset Mix

Pie chart:
- Large Cap Equity 30%
- Fixed Income 27%
- Real Estate 10%
- International Equity 8%
- Hedge Funds 6%
- Private Equity 6%
- Small Cap Equity 6%
- Cash Reserves 5%
- Emerging Market Equity 2%

Asset Composition
Stocks	46%
Fixed Income	27%
Cash	5%
Other	22%

Return/Risk
Expected Return	8.2%
Expected Income	2.5%
Standard Deviation	8.6%
Negative Return Frequency:	
12-Month Period	17.1%
60-Month Period	1.7%

The correlation matrix from Table 38 and Table 39 illustrate the changing nature of statistical input needed by mean variance math optimizers. For example, Table 38 shows a -0.39 for the emerging market and hedge fund correlation while Table 39 has the correlation at +0.65. This changing nature of MPT statistical input indicates uncertainty with mean variance optimizer solutions in real life.

Table 38. Typical Historical Correlation Matrix. Data from 1970 to 2001.
(Source: Glenmede, Private Wealth Management Summit, San Juan Puerto Rico, April 18-20, 2002).

Efficient Frontier Analysis

Expected Return and Risk Assumptions

Asset Class	Expected Return	Historical (1970-2001) Return	St Dev	Periods	Maximum Weight	Minimum Weight	Inflation	Cash	Tax-Free Govts	Interm TIPS	Munis	Interm Bonds	High Yield	Non-US Bonds	Large Cap	Small Cap	Int'l Equity	Emerg Markets	Hedge Fund	Private Equity	Real Estate
1. Inflation	3.0%	5.0%	3.2%	32	-	-	1.00	0.61	(0.18)	0.91	(0.20)	(0.24)	(0.38)	0.04	(0.28)	0.02	(0.21)	0.13	0.29	(0.05)	0.35
2. Cash	4.3%	6.6%	2.6%	32	5%	3%		1.00	0.36	0.56	0.32	0.33	(0.02)	0.31	(0.03)	0.00	(0.13)	(0.02)	0.57	(0.14)	0.36
3. Intermediate Govt	5.0%	8.7%	5.5%	32	0%	0%			1.00	(0.10)	0.99	1.00	0.56	0.63	0.28	0.21	(0.03)	(0.09)	0.75	(0.32)	0.19
4. TII (Inflation-Ind)	6.0%	8.6%	3.5%	32	10%	0%				1.00	(0.13)	(0.16)	(0.41)	(0.08)	(0.41)	(0.06)	(0.33)	(0.30)	0.71	(0.36)	0.45
5. Munis	4.3%	7.1%	4.3%	32	35%	0%					1.00	0.99	0.60	0.64	0.29	0.24	(0.02)	(0.01)	0.69	(0.29)	0.20
6. US Govt/Credit	6.0%	8.7%	5.7%	29	0%	0%						1.00	0.62	0.63	0.36	0.27	0.07	(0.07)	0.73	(0.31)	0.19
7. High Yield	8.0%	9.3%	12.6%	32	10%	0%							1.00	0.49	0.55	0.64	0.33	0.26	0.10	0.01	0.29
8. Non-US Bonds	7.0%	9.1%	9.2%	17	0%	0%								1.00	0.34	0.10	0.60	(0.06)	0.17	(0.16)	(0.05)
9. Large Cap	9.0%	12.0%	16.7%	32	100%	0%									1.00	0.76	0.55	0.25	(0.09)	0.43	0.26
10. Small Cap	10.0%	13.5%	19.2%	32	10%	0%										1.00	0.37	0.47	0.04	0.35	0.60
11. Int'l Equity	9.0%	11.0%	22.4%	32	15%	0%											1.00	0.52	(0.44)	0.40	0.13
12. Emerg Mkts	10.0%	8.6%	31.8%	17	5%	0%												1.00	(0.39)	0.43	0.08
13. Hedge Funds	12.0%	14.5%	6.0%	12	6%	0%													1.00	(0.27)	0.50
14. Private Eqty	14.0%	17.8%	21.2%	22	6%	0%														1.00	0.08
15. Real Estate	9.0%	11.9%	8.1%	24	10%	0%															1.00

Definition: Correlation Coefficient is a measure of the linear relationship between two variables

Data Sources: Historical Returns, standard deviations, and correlations from Ibbotson Associates, Venture Economics and FactSet

Table 39. Example Asset Allocation Correlations.
(Source: Hammond, P. B., "Reverse Asset Allocation Alternatives at the Core", TIA-Cref Asset Management, Second Quarter, 2007).

EXHIBIT 1: ASSET CLASS CORRELATIONS

	U.S. Equity	International Equity	Emerging Mkt Equity	Absolute Return	Equity Hedge Funds	Venture Capital	Private Equity	REITs	Real Estate	Commodities	U.S. Bonds Govt	U.S. Bonds All	U.S. Bonds TIPS	Cash
U.S. Equity	1.00	0.65	0.45	0.50	0.85	0.35	0.70	0.55	0.10	-0.25	0.35	0.30	0.35	0.35
International Equity	0.65	1.00	0.60	0.55	0.55	0.30	0.60	0.40	0.15	-0.10	0.20	0.20	0.20	0.20
Emerging Mkt Equity	0.45	0.60	1.00	0.50	0.65	0.35	0.30	0.20	-0.30	-0.05	-0.20	-0.15	-0.10	0.00
Absolute Return	0.50	0.55	0.50	1.00	0.65	0.10	0.35	0.55	-0.05	-0.05	0.10	0.15	0.15	0.20
Equity Hedge Funds	0.85	0.55	0.65	0.65	1.00	0.50	0.60	0.50	0.00	-0.05	0.10	0.15	0.25	0.35
Venture Capital	0.35	0.30	0.35	0.10	0.50	1.00	0.65	-0.05	0.15	0.20	-0.30	-0.25	-0.15	0.05
Private Equity	0.70	0.60	0.30	0.35	0.60	0.65	1.00	0.20	0.20	-0.05	-0.15	-0.10	0.05	0.25
REITs	0.55	0.40	0.20	0.55	0.50	-0.05	0.20	1.00	0.00	-0.20	0.35	0.30	0.30	0.20
Real Estate	0.10	0.15	-0.30	-0.05	0.00	0.15	0.20	0.00	1.00	-0.05	0.00	0.00	0.20	0.40
Commodities	-0.25	-0.10	-0.05	-0.05	-0.05	0.20	-0.05	-0.20	-0.05	1.00	-0.20	-0.10	-0.20	-0.20
U.S. Bonds Govt	0.35	0.20	-0.20	0.10	0.10	-0.30	-0.15	0.35	0.00	-0.20	1.00	1.00	0.75	0.50
U.S. Bonds All	0.30	0.20	-0.15	0.15	0.15	-0.25	-0.10	0.30	0.00	-0.10	1.00	1.00	0.75	0.45
U.S. Bonds TIPS	0.35	0.20	-0.10	0.15	0.25	-0.15	0.05	0.30	0.20	-0.20	0.75	0.75	1.00	0.75
Cash	0.35	0.20	0.00	0.20	0.35	0.05	0.25	0.20	0.40	-0.20	0.50	0.45	0.75	1.00

These estimates, which are drawn from Leibowitz and Bova (2004), are used for illustration only and may or may not reflect current expectations for any or all asset classes. Source: Morgan Stanley Research

Hammond examines portfolios of alternate investments or hedge funds, for institutional investors. (Source: Hammond, P.B., "Reverse Asset

Allocation: Alternatives at the Core", TIAA-Cref Asset Management, Second Quarter 2007). Employing returns, standard deviations, and correlation coefficients the Reverse Asset Allocation article defines three portfolios for comparison. "A" is 60% equity and 40% bonds, a standard allocation. Optimal portfolio B is obtained when international equity is included with roughly the same returns computed. Optimal portfolio C is obtained when alternative assets are added and has a higher return with the same risk as portfolio A or B, see Table 40.

Table 40. Description of 3 Efficient Portfolios.
(Source: Hammond, P.B., "Reverse Asset Allocation: Alternatives at the Core", TIAA-Cref Asset Management, Second Quarter 2007).

EXHIBIT 2: EFFICIENT PORTFOLIOS A,B,C

	A	B	C
U.S. Equity	60	45	0
International Equity	-	18	0
Emerging Mkt Equity	-	-	10
Absolute Return	-	-	0
Equity Hedge Funds	-	-	0
Venture Capital	-	-	24
Private Equity	-	-	8
REITs	-	-	31
Real Estate	-	-	20
Commodities	-	-	7
U.S. Bonds All	40	37	0
Cash	0	0	0
Expected Return*	5.85	5.95	8.19
Beta-Based Structural Alpha	0.67	0.88	4.30
Standard Deviation	11.17	11.17	11.17
Sharpe Ratio	0.52	0.53	0.73
Beta	0.65	0.64	0.44

* Expected returns are calculated using mean-variance analysis. Optimizer results involving alternative assets may be highly sensitive to changes in the input assumptions.

In cases where zero appears for an asset class, the model was allowed to consider the asset, but the efficient portfolio assigned a zero weight to it. In cases where no number appears, it means the model was not allowed to consider the asset in the optimization.

Source: TIAA-CREF Asset Management

Other portfolios are computed with constrained assed allocations of 3.75% (D), 5. % (E), 6.25% (F) and 7.5% (G), see Table 41. As expected, the higher the constraining % the higher the computed return at the same risk or standard deviation value. Constraining the optimizer allocation essentially limits the computer answer to the input constraint. Constraints may indicate problems with the input data and constrained solutions should be examined carefully.

Table 41. Description of Efficient Portfolios.
(Source: Hammond, P.B., "Reverse Asset Allocation: Alternatives at the Core", TIAA-Cref Asset Management, Second Quarter 2007).

EXHIBIT 7: EFFICIENT PORTFOLIOS B–G*

	B	C	D	E	F	G
U.S. Equity	45	0	40	37	34	30
International Equity	18	0	12	10	8	5
Emerging Mkt Equity	–	10	3.75	5	6.25	7.50
Absolute Return	–	0	3.75	5	6.25	7.50
Equity Hedge Funds	–	0	3.75	5	6.25	7.50
Venture Capital	–	24	3.75	5	6.25	7.50
Private Equity	–	8	3.75	5	6.25	7.50
REITs	–	31	3.75	5	6.25	7.50
Real Estate	–	20	3.75	5	6.25	7.50
Commodities	–	7	3.75	5	6.25	7.50
U.S. Bonds All	37	0	18	13	9	5
Cash	0	0	0	0	0	0
Expected Return	5.95	8.19	6.69	6.89	7.07	7.23
Beta-Based Structural Alpha	0.88	4.30	1.56	1.80	2.05	2.31
Standard Deviation	11.17	11.17	11.17	11.17	11.17	11.17
Sharpe Ratio	0.53	0.73	0.60	0.62	0.63	0.65
Beta	0.64	0.44	0.55	0.64	0.63	0.61

* **PORTFOLIO COMPOSITION:**
 B U.S. Equities, International Equities, U.S. Bonds, Cash
 C All Asset Classes
 D 30% to Alternatives
 E 40% to Alternatives
 F 50% to Alternatives
 G 60% to Alternatives

Some allocations may not add up to 100% due to rounding. Source: TIAA-CREF Asset Management

Return vs. risk is illustrated in Figure 18 for portfolios B and C and various asset classes.

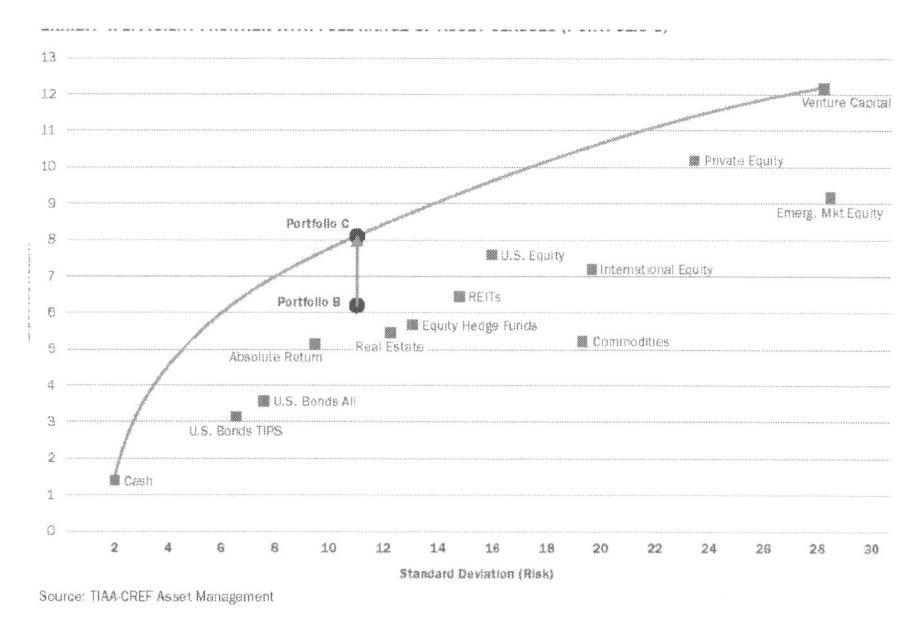

[Figure: Efficient Frontier chart with asset classes plotted by Standard Deviation (Risk) on x-axis and return on y-axis. Points shown include: Cash, U.S. Bonds TIPS, U.S. Bonds All, Absolute Return, Real Estate, Equity Hedge Funds, REITs, Commodities, U.S. Equity, International Equity, Emerg. Mkt Equity, Private Equity, Venture Capital, Portfolio B, Portfolio C. Source: TIAA-CREF Asset Management.]

(Source: Hammond, P.B., "Reverse Asset Allocation: Alternatives at the Core", TIAA-Cref Asset Management, Second Quarter 2007).

Figure 18. Efficient Frontier With Many Asset Classes.

Example of Expected Return for Different Stock/Bond Ratios

(adapted from Montecito Capital Management, http://mcapitalmgt.com/html/assetallocation.htm).

The return for different stock/bond ratios is illustrated in Table 42. Because stocks usually produce higher return than bonds, the expected return decreases with higher bond ratio portfolios. Risk in terms of standard deviation is used to bracket the expected return. For a 60/40 stock/bond ratio portfolio the expected return is 11.6% per year. For this 60/40 ratio using one standard deviation corrects the return by both a plus 6% and a minus 6% for a 5-year horizon. Thus the expected return is not simply 11.6% but is 17.6% to 5.6% over a 5-year time frame. The uncertainty or risk correction, to the mean, decreases over longer time horizons according to this data.

When other asset classes are added to the stock/bond classes the portfolio return generally increases and portfolio risk decreases, see the lower part b of Table 42. For example, portfolio 7 has 40% US equity, 20% international equity, 30% US bonds and 10% international bonds. The hypothetical portfolio return increases from 10.96% (for portfolio

1 with 60/40) to 11.12%; the risk decreases from 9.94 to 7.87%. These kinds of analyses sometimes guide portfolio construction. But the small changes from the baseline are suspicious. Remember that average daily return changes in the S&P500 index can be about 1%.

Table 42. Expected Return of Stock/Bond with Risk Corrections and With Added Asset Classes, 1993.

a) STOCKS, BONDS, ALLOCATION AND STANDARD DEVIATION: (1993)

Stock/Bond Ratio	Expected Return	Change to expected return, both positive and negative, for a 1 Year Horizon	Change to expected return, both positive and negative, for a 5 Year Horizon	Change to expected return, both positive and negative, for a 10 Year Horizon
100%/0%	14.0%	20.0%	8.9%	6.3%
90/10	13.4	16.3	8.2	5.8
80/20	12.8	16.6	7.4	5.3
70/30	12.2	15.0	6.7	4.7
60/40	11.6	13.4	6.0	4.2
50/50	11.0	11.8	5.2	3.7
40/60	10.4	10.3	4.6	3.3
30/70	9.8	8.9	4.0	2.8
10/90	8.6	6.6	3.0	2.1
0/100	8.0	6.0	2.7	1.9

b) ASSET ALLOCATION 1986- 1994 (7 Portfolio Allocation % Allocation between 5 Asset Classes)

Portfolio	1	2	3	4	5	6	7
US Equity	60	50	40	40	40	50	40
International Equity	0	10	10	20	20	10	20
US Bonds	40	40	40	40	30	30	30
International Bonds Unhedged	0	0	10	0	10	0	0
International Bonds Hedged	0	0	0	0	0	10	10
Portfolio Return, %	10.96	11.13	11.49	11.3	11.66	10.95	11.12
Portfolio Risk, %	9.94	8.76	8.67	8.48	8.33	8.37	7.87

(Source: Montecito Capital Management, http://mcapitalmgt.com/html/assetallocation.htm).

Buffet Large Capitalization Growth Study

Warren Buffet is a well-known investor who buys and holds companies. Martin and Puthenpurackal analyzed his investments from 1980 to 2003; see Table 43. They analyzed his holdings from SEC filings and concluded that he has a concentrated large-cap portfolio. They found that the largest 5 holdings account for about 70% his portfolio. The concentrated portion of his portfolio beat the S&P500 in 20 out of the last 24 years, from 1980 to 2003, by an average of 12.24%. Over this period the S&P500 average return was 14.85%. Buffet's average return is significantly better than the average return of most money managers. Buffet is known for his ability to buy companies at low prices. In contrast to Buffet's concentrated portfolio approach, it is common investment practice to hold fully diversified portfolios.

Table 43. Annual Performance Summary of Berkshire Hathaway Stock, Stock Portfolio and S&P500 Comparison, 1980 to 2003.
(Source: Martin, G.S., Puthenpurackl, J, "Imitation is the Sincerest Form of Flattery: Warren Buffet and Berkshire Hathaway", August 13, 2005. Available at SSRN: <http://ssrn.com/abstract=806246>); S&P500 returns are from the 2003 Berkshire Hathaway Annual Report.

Year	B-H stock return	No. of holdings in portfolio	Stock portfolio largest 5 holdings	Return of largest 5 holdings	S&P500 index return	Return largest 5-S&P500 return
1980	31.06%	102	48.3%	20.09%	32.30%	-12.21%
1981	30.64	27	61.3	32.30	-5.00	37.30
1982	38.50	22	68.4	54.79	21.40	33.39
1983	69.33	14	86.1	37.80	22.40	15.40
1984	-2.83%	16	77.1	11.66	6.10	5.56
1985	91.84	13	83.6	88.76	31.60	57.16
1986	14.17	11	95.0	24.21	18.6	5.61
1987	4.61	13	96.2	22.36	5.10	17.26
1988	59.32	16	91.0	16.07	16.60	-0.53
1989	84.57	10	94.0	53.96	31.70	22.26
1990	-23.05	11	91.8	4.87	-3.10	7.97
1991	35.58	12	88.6	48.76	30.50	18.26
1992	29.83	14	83.1	20.92	7.60	13.32

1993	38.94	23	74.3	13.45	10.10	3.35
1994	24.96	29	69.5	17.04	1.30	15.74
1995	57.35	30	70.9	47.62	37.60	10.02
1996	6.23	30	72.2	36.92	23.00	13.92
1997	34.90	30	72.8	40.89	33.40	7.49
1998	52.17	33	77.3	13.80	28.60	-14.80
1999	-19.86	35	78.4	7.14	21.00	13.86
2000	26.56	41	76.3	15.57	-9.10	24.67
2001	6.48	34	76.2	-10.50	-11.90	1.40
2002	-3.77	35	74.8	2.52	-22.10	24.62
2003	15.81	32	74.1	29.26	28.70	0.56
Average	29.31	26.4	78.39	27.09	14.85	12.24

8. Risk Evaluation

An investment questionnaire is needed to assess risk tolerance and to quantify financial resources. The former is needed to mange the investment account. The latter information is needed to help satisfy the Patriot Act that requires advisors to know their customers.

Risk management is difficult to accomplish. Buy-and-hold ceases to manage risk after the initial allocation investment until the next meeting. Humans are driven by both logic and emotion.

Logic or Emotion

Many people have difficulty estimating risks of future events. This makes logical and emotionless decisions that much harder. Logical and emotional examples are listed below.

Many people think future probability is related to past events, consider:

Evelyn is 33, single, bright and majored in education. At college she worked against police injustice and demonstrated against the Iraq war. Which is more likely?

- Evelyn is a wealth-manager _____
- Evelyn is a teacher and leads a girl scout troop _____

Joe is 40, married with 2 children. His father and grandfather were physicists. His hobby is amateur radio. Which is more likely?

- Joe is an engineer _____
- Joe is a barber _____

Story or Data

Many people believe stories and others believe data, consider:

An analyst highly recommends purchasing stock in a new fast growing Internet company in India (story).

A research report indicates that 75 % of new technology Indian issues are lower after 12 months (data).

Would you invest in this stock based on the analyst tip (story) or not based on the 75% loss research report (data)? _____

Fear of Losing

The psychological value of a loss is greater than the value of a gain. Many people don't want to sell a losing position.

One way to sell a losing position is to decide what to buy with the cash. To sell a losing position, I would buy: _____

Estimate

It is easier for people to estimate the probability of single events rather than a series of events. For example,

You hear about a new car company that is fueled by sugar cane extract, Hot Brazil Car, and are thinking about investing in it.

You think the new company has an 85% chance of building a prototype car. After a prototype is built you think the probability of producing the car is 85%.

Would you buy it? _____

The overall probability of success of producing the car is = $(0.85)^2$ = 0.72%. But, if you consider two more steps of financing and marketing, each with 85% probability, the end probability drops to 52%. This probability is, most likely, a lot lower than initially thought.

Small Samples

Consider rolling one die five times and a different die 100 times.

- Die #1 is tossed 5 times and lands on "1" 2 times.
- Die #2 is tossed 100 times and lands on "1" 100 times.

Die 1 is not tossed enough times to get stationary, or accurate, statistics. Die 2 is loaded. A legitimate die should land on "1" about 1/6 of the time.

Sample Risk Tolerance Questionnaire

A risk tolerance questionnaire is helpful to quantify your investment time horizon and your tolerance for risk. An example is given below. (Adapted from:" Canadian Institute of Financial Planners", <www.advisor.ca/practice/running_your_business/article.jsp?content=20060912_113157_1560>, September 2006)

Circle the response that best describes you. Remember that risk tolerance is largely subjective, so there is no right or wrong answer.

Time Horizon

1. What is your current age?

    a) 65 or older.
    b) 60 to 64.
    c) 55 to 59.
    d) 40 to 54.
    e) Under 40.

2. When do you expect to need to withdraw cash from your investment portfolio?

    a) In less than 1 year.
    b) Within 1 to 2 years.
    c) Within 2 to 5 years.
    d) Within 5 to 15 years.
    e) Not for at least 15 years.

Financial Resources

3. How many months of current living expenses could you cover with your present savings and liquid, short-term investments, before you would have to draw on your investment portfolio?

    a) Less than 3 months.
    b) 3 to 6 months.
    c) 6 to 18 months.
    d) More than 18 months.

4. Over the next few years, what do you expect will happen to your income?

    a) It will probably decrease substantially.
    b) It will probably decrease slightly.
    c) It will probably stay the same.
    d) It will probably increase slightly.
    e) It will probably increase substantially.

5. What percentage of your gross annual income have you been able to save in recent years?

    a) None.
    b) 1 to 10%.
    c) 10 to 20%
    d) 20 to 30%
    e) More than 30%

6. Over the next few years, what do you expect will happen to your rate of savings?

- a) It will probably decrease substantially.
- b) It will probably decrease slightly.
- c) It will probably stay the same.
- d) It will probably increase slightly.
- e) It will probably increase substantially.

Risk emotional tolerance

7. What are your return expectations for your portfolio?

- a) I don't care if my portfolio keeps pace with inflation; I just want to preserve my capital.
- b) My return should keep pace with inflation, with minimum volatility.
- c) My return should be slightly more than inflation, with only moderate volatility.
- d) My return should significantly exceed inflation, even if this could mean significant volatility.

8. How would you characterize your personality?

- a) I'm a pessimist. I always expect the worst.
- b) I'm anxious. No matter what you say, I'll worry.
- c) I'm cautious but open to new ideas. Convince me.
- d) I'm objective. Show me the pros and cons and I can make a decision and live with it.
- e) I'm optimistic. Things always work out in the end.

9. When monitoring your investments over time, what do you think you will tend to focus on?

- a) Individual investments that are doing poorly.
- b) Individual investments that are doing very well.
- c) The recent results of my overall portfolio.
- d) The long-term performance of my overall portfolio.

10. **Suppose you had $1,000,000 to invest and the choice of 5 different portfolios with a range of possible outcomes after a single year. Which of the following portfolios would you feel most comfortable investing in?**

   a) Portfolio A, which could have a balance ranging from $990,000 to $1,003,000 at the end of the year.
   b) Portfolio B, which could have a balance ranging from $980,000 to $1,006,000 at the end of the year.
   c) Portfolio C, which could have a balance ranging from $960,000 to $1,100,000 at the end of the year.
   d) Portfolio D, which could have a balance ranging from $920,000 to $1,200,000 at the end of the year.
   e) Portfolio E, which could have a balance ranging from $840,000 to $1,400,000 at the end of the year.

11. **If the value of your investment portfolio dropped by 20% in one year, what would you do? A market loss of 20% is typically 1 year out of 4.**

   a) Fire my investment advisor.
   b) Move my money to more conservative investments immediately to reduce the potential for future loss.
   c) Monitor the situation, and if it looks like things could continue to deteriorate, move some money to more conservative investments.
   d) Consult with my investment advisor to ensure that my asset allocation is correct, and then ride it out.
   e) Consider investing more because prices are so low.

12. **Which of the following risks or events do you fear most?**

   a) A loss of principal over any period of 1 year or less.
   b) A rate of inflation that exceeds my rate of return over the long term, because it will erode the purchasing power of my money.
   c) Portfolio performance that is insufficient to meet my goals.
   d) Portfolio performance that is consistently less than industry benchmarks.
   e) A missed investment opportunity that could have yielded higher returns over the long term, even though it entailed higher risk.

Interpretation of results provides an investment time horizon and a risk level.

9. Example Investment Proposal: Hypothetical Case Study

November 19, 2007

This investment proposal is representative of mean variance optimization proposals. If a HNW individual were to ask three CFP or CFA exam-pass designated Wealth Managers/financial planners to submit investment proposals, it is likely they would be similar. Differences would be due to different assumptions and constraints. Re-balancing the portfolio is assumed to be once a year.

Background: a hypothetical investor, Mr. Joe Smith, is 47 years old, was born January 1,1960, and plans to retire in November 2025. His goal upon retiring is to receive $80,000 (adjusted for inflation) per year from his investments. Withdrawal from the IRA begins upon retirement. (Financial goals column) beginning in 2025. His current Sep IRA is worth $1,000,000 and he is able to add $20,000 per year adjusted upward each year indexed for 2.5% inflation. Typical asset allocation software is employed and three-year average statistics of alpha, beta, variance, and correlation coefficients are used in the analysis. The mutual fund allocation is constrained to be 5% for 10 funds of the 20 funds chosen to gain more diversification. The analysis shows that $1 million grows to about $36.2 million over the 43 year period at about 8.47% per year net of fees. The management fee is included at 0.75% per year, and fees are paid outside of the account. This makes the net of fee return larger than it would have been otherwise. Upon retirement, his federal income tax bracket is assumed to be 33% and Ohio state bracket is 6.56% and taxes are paid on only the amount withdrawn each year.

A (different) risk tolerance analysis is listed in Table 44. The client has an aggressive risk tolerance. An efficient frontier analysis of the proposed new portfolio of Qualified Assets (tax-deferred) is illustrated in Figure 19. A pie chart of the proposed asset allocation is shown in Figure 20. An asset mix comparison of present and proposed portfolio is shown in Figure 21and Table 45. The forecast asset values are provided in Table 46. Table 47shows the plan implementation.

Disclaimer: This asset allocation analysis is provided for informational purposes only. Actual investment results may differ from the projected performance. Information used is considered reliable, but may not be accurate or complete, and should not be relied upon. This does not guarantee actual performance or provide tax or legal advice. This is not a solicitation to buy or sell securities. The deduction of advisory fees, brokerage or other commissions, and any other expenses may not be reflected in the analysis. The results portrayed reflect the reinvestment of dividends and earnings.

Table 44. Risk Tolerance Analysis.

No.	Question	Response
1	Expected Return. My desired investment return is above average.	4
2	Risk Tolerance. I am willing to bear an above-average level of investment risk (volatility). I can accept occasional years with negative investment returns.	4
3	Holding Period. I am willing to maintain investment positions over a reasonably long period of time (generally considered 5 years or more).	5
4	Liquidity. I do not need to be able to readily convert my investments into cash. Aside from my portfolio, I have adequate liquid net worth to meet major near-term expenses.	5
5	Ease of Management. I want to be very actively involved in the monitoring and decision-making required to manage my investments.	3
6	Dependents. There are none or only a few dependents that rely on my income and my investment portfolio for support.	5
7	Income Source. My major Source of income is adequate, predictable and steadily growing.	5
8	Insurance Coverage. I have an adequate insurance coverage.	5
9	Investment Experience. I have prior investment experience with stocks, bonds, and international investments. I understand the concept of investment risk.	5
10	Debt/Credit. My debt level is low and my credit history is excellent.	5

Responses: 1 = Strongly Disagree; 5 = Strongly Agree; Your Risk Profile: Aggressive

A risk tolerance analysis helps one approach to select a suitable portfolio. A range of portfolios on the Efficient Frontier that may be appropriate for this risk profile.

The computed efficient frontier, as of November 2007, with 3-year averaged statistical data is illustrated in **Figure 19**. Conservative, moderate, and aggressive risk levels are indicated at risk below 13.9%, between 13.9% and 14.8%, and higher than 14.8% respectively. Notice that the present portfolio of 100% Vanguard 500 index fund has a higher return than the efficient frontier with a risk level of about 15.25%.

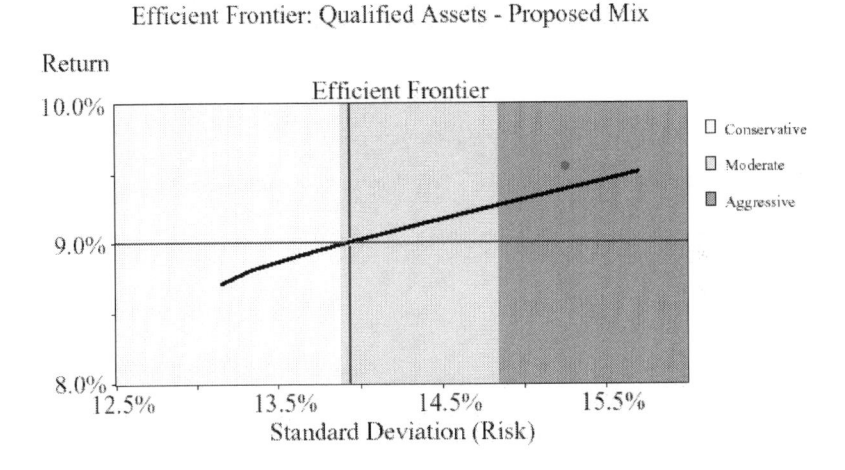

Efficient Frontier: Qualified Assets - Proposed Mix

Figure 19. Efficient Frontier and Three Risk Levels.

This example illustrates the assumption that returns are constant and don't vary from year to year and that investing results can be simulated by computer. The reallocation away from the Vanguard 500 index to 20 funds accomplishes the following: gross return decreases, standard deviation decreases, and yield increases from 0.9% to 1.93%, see Figure 20.

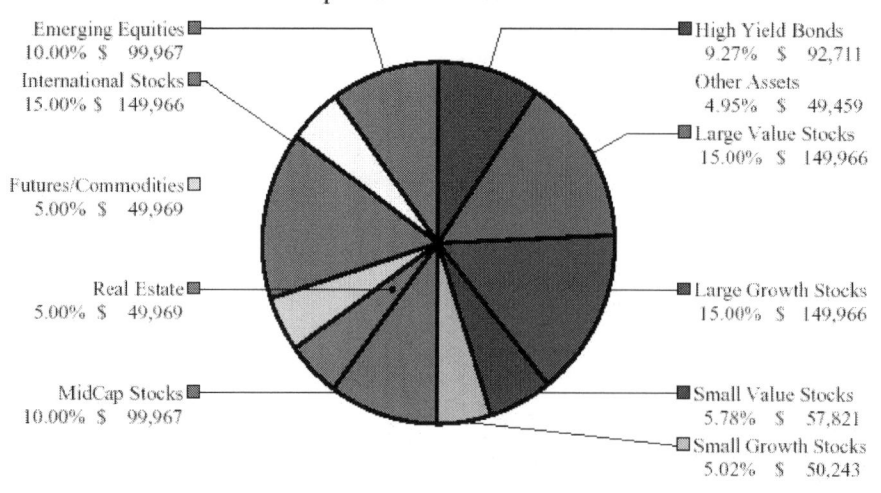

Proposed Asset Allocation

- Emerging Equities 10.00% $ 99,967
- International Stocks 15.00% $ 149,966
- Futures/Commodities 5.00% $ 49,969
- Real Estate 5.00% $ 49,969
- MidCap Stocks 10.00% $ 99,967
- High Yield Bonds 9.27% $ 92,711
- Other Assets 4.95% $ 49,459
- Large Value Stocks 15.00% $ 149,966
- Large Growth Stocks 15.00% $ 149,966
- Small Value Stocks 5.78% $ 57,821
- Small Growth Stocks 5.02% $ 50,243

	•Present	+Proposed
Expected Gross Return	10.30%	9.76%
Expected Return	9.55%	9.01%
Std Deviation (Risk)	15.25%	13.94%
Sharpe Ratio	0.46	0.47
Yield	0.90%	1.93%

Figure 20. Proposed Asset Allocation Pie Chart.

A pie-shaped graphic that illustrate the reallocation from 1 fund to 20 funds is shown in Figure 21.

Asset Mix Comparison - Composite Assets
Present Asset Mix   Proposed Asset Mix

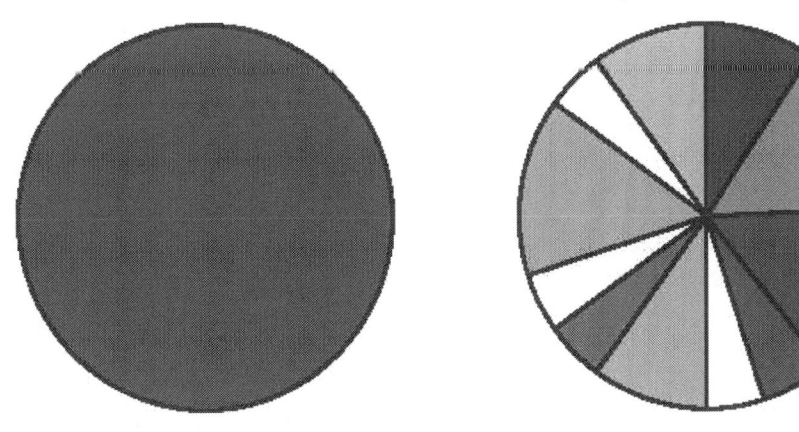

Figure 21. Asset Mix Comparison.

Table 45. Proposed Asset Allocation.

	Present Asset Mix		Proposed Asset Mix		Adjustment
■ High Yield Bonds	$ 0	-%	$ 92,711	9.27%	$ 92,711
■ Large Value Stocks	0	-	149,966	15.00	149,966
■ Large Growth Stocks	1,000,000	100.00	149,966	15.00	-850,034
■ Small Value Stocks	0	-	57,821	5.78	57,821
▨ Small Growth Stocks	0	-	50,243	5.02	50,243
■ MidCap Stocks	0	-	99,967	10.00	99,967
■ Real Estate	0	-	49,969	5.00	49,969
▨ Futures/Commodities	0	-	49,969	5.00	49,969
■ International Stocks	0	-	149,966	15.00	149,966
☐ International Bonds	0	-	49,459	4.95	49,459
■ Emerging Equities	0	-	99,967	10.00	99,967
Total	$ 1,000,000	100.00%	$ 1,000,000	100.00%	
Before-Tax Gross Return		10.30%		9.76%	
Before-Tax Net Return		9.55%		9.01%	
After-Tax Net Return		9.55%		9.01%	
Std Deviation (Risk)		15.25%		13.94%	
Sharpe Ratio		0.46		0.47	
Yield		0.90%		1.93%	
Income (Annual $)	$ 9,000		$ 19,331		

Forecast asset values, starting November 2007 and ending November 2050 are indicated in Table 46.

Table 46. Forecast Asset Values.

Date	Asset value	Addt'l contrib	Current income	Capital gains	With-drawal	Taxes	Mgmt fees in/out acct	Net change
Nov-07	1,000,000	20,000	19,331	70,766	0	0	7,500	110,097
Nov-08	1,110,097	20,500	21,459	78,557	0	0	8,326	120,516
Nov-09	1,230,613	21,013	23,789	87,086	0	0	9,230	131,887
Nov-10	1,362,500	21,538	26,338	96,419	0	0	10,219	144,295
Nov-11	1,506,796	22,076	29,128	106,630	0	0	11,301	157,834
Nov-12	1,664,630	22,628	32,179	117,799	0	0	12,485	172,606
Nov-13	1,837,236	23,194	35,516	130,014	0	0	13,779	188,723
Nov-14	2,025,959	23,774	39,164	143,369	0	0	15,195	206,307
Nov-15	2,232,266	24,368	43,152	157,969	0	0	16,742	225,488
Nov-16	2,457,754	24,977	47,511	173,925	0	0	18,433	246,414
Nov-17	2,704,168	25,602	52,274	191,363	0	0	20,281	269,239
Nov-18	2,973,407	26,242	57,479	210,416	0	0	22,301	294,137
Nov-19	3,267,544	26,898	63,165	231,231	0	0	24,507	321,294
Nov-20	3,588,837	27,570	69,376	253,968	0	0	26,916	350,914
Nov-21	3,939,751	28,259	76,159	278,800	0	0	29,548	383,219
Nov-22	4,322,970	28,966	83,567	305,919	0	0	32,422	418,453
Nov-23	4,741,423	29,690	91,656	335,532	0	0	35,561	456,878
Nov-24	5,198,301	30,432	100,488	367,863	0	0	38,987	498,784
Nov-25	5,697,084	0	110,130	403,160	124,773	49,360	42,728	388,518
Nov-26	6,085,602	0	117,641	430,654	127,892	50,594	45,642	420,402
Nov-27	6,506,004	0	125,768	460,404	131,089	51,859	48,795	455,082
Nov-28	6,961,087	0	134,565	492,608	134,367	53,155	52,208	492,806
Nov-29	7,453,893	0	144,091	527,482	137,726	54,484	55,904	533,848
Nov-30	7,987,741	0	154,411	565,260	141,169	55,846	59,908	578,503
Nov-31	8,566,243	0	165,594	606,199	144,698	57,243	64,247	627,095
Nov-32	9,193,338	0	177,716	650,576	148,316	58,674	68,950	679,977
Nov-33	9,873,315	0	190,861	698,695	152,023	60,140	74,050	737,533
Nov-34	10,610,847	0	205,118	750,887	155,824	61,644	79,581	800,182
Nov-35	11,411,029	0	220,587	807,513	159,720	63,185	85,583	868,380
Nov-36	12,279,409	0	237,373	868,965	163,713	64,765	92,096	942,625
Nov-37	13,222,034	0	255,595	935,670	167,805	66,384	99,165	1,023,460
Nov-38	14,245,494	0	275,380	1,008,097	172,001	68,043	106,841	1,111,476
Nov-39	15,356,970	0	296,866	1,086,751	176,301	69,744	115,177	1,207,316
Nov-40	16,564,286	0	320,204	1,172,188	180,708	71,488	124,232	1,311,684
Nov-41	17,875,971	0	345,560	1,265,011	185,226	73,275	134,070	1,425,346

Nov-42	19,301,316	0	373,114	1,365,877	189,856	75,107	144,760	1,549,134
Nov-43	20,850,451	0	403,060	1,475,503	194,603	76,985	156,378	1,683,960
Nov-44	22,534,411	0	435,613	1,594,670	199,468	78,909	169,008	1,830,815
Nov-45	24,365,226	0	471,004	1,724,230	204,455	80,882	182,739	1,990,779
Nov-46	26,356,005	0	509,488	1,865,109	209,566	82,904	197,670	2,165,031
Nov-47	28,521,036	0	551,340	2,018,320	214,805	84,977	213,908	2,354,855
Nov-48	30,875,891	0	596,862	2,184,963	220,175	87,101	231,569	2,561,650
Nov-49	33,437,541	0	646,381	2,366,241	225,680	89,279	250,782	2,786,942
Nov-50	36,224,483	0	0	0	0	0	0	0
Sum=		447,727	8,376,054	30,662,658	4,261,956	1,686,030	3,249,724	35,224,483
	Final asset value	Addt'l contrib	Sum income	Sum capital gains	Sum withdrawal	Sum taxes	Sum mgmt fees in acct	Net acct gain included

After tax net return from 2007 to 2050 + 8.47 % (= exp {1/43 ln [(36224483 - 3,249724)/1,000,000]} - 1.), where the cumulative management fee is subtracted from the final asset value.

Product recommendations for the qualified assets are shown in Figure 22. The asset classes are identified in the chart. Mutual funds, variable annuities, and variable life insurance may be part of this recommendation, and are sold only by prospectus. Please read the prospectus for information concerning surrender periods, penalties, fees, and any other internal expenses. A prospectus can be obtained from your investment advisor.

Dr. Gary J. Harloff, Ph.D

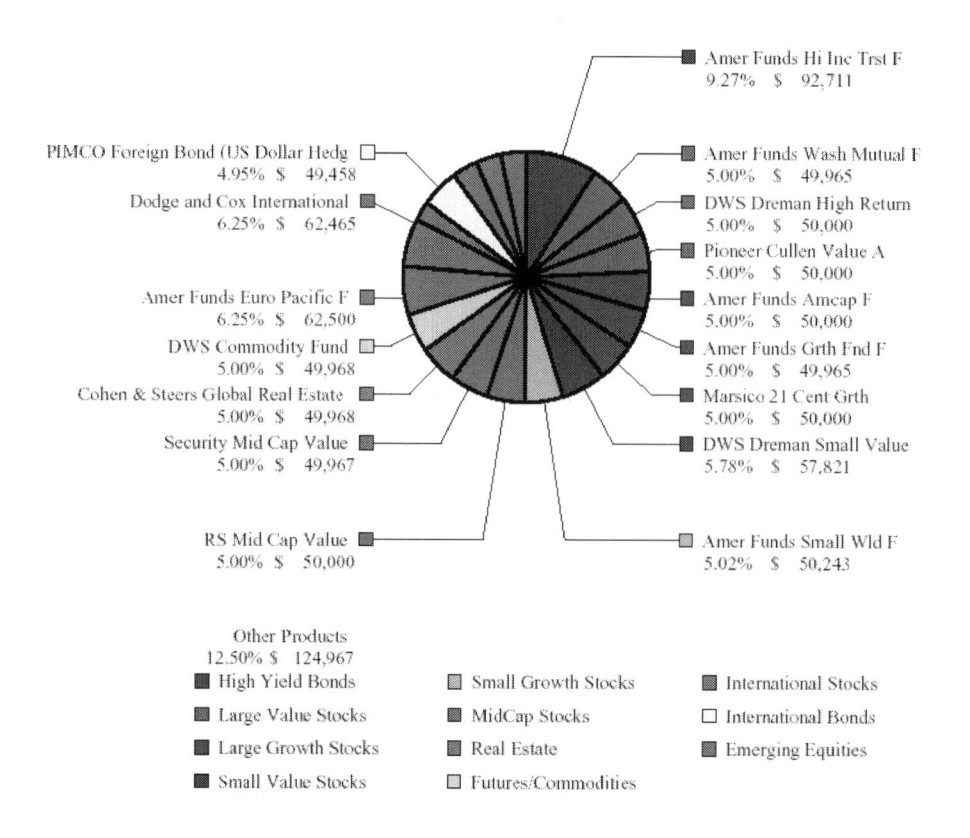

Figure 22. Proposed Asset Allocation Pie Chart.

Pie chart segments:
- Amer Funds Hi Inc Trst F — 9.27% $ 92,711
- Amer Funds Wash Mutual F — 5.00% $ 49,965
- DWS Dreman High Return — 5.00% $ 50,000
- Pioneer Cullen Value A — 5.00% $ 50,000
- Amer Funds Amcap F — 5.00% $ 50,000
- Amer Funds Grth Fnd F — 5.00% $ 49,965
- Marsico 21 Cent Grth — 5.00% $ 50,000
- DWS Dreman Small Value — 5.78% $ 57,821
- Amer Funds Small Wld F — 5.02% $ 50,243
- RS Mid Cap Value — 5.00% $ 50,000
- Security Mid Cap Value — 5.00% $ 49,967
- Cohen & Steers Global Real Estate — 5.00% $ 49,968
- DWS Commodity Fund — 5.00% $ 49,968
- Amer Funds Euro Pacific F — 6.25% $ 62,500
- Dodge and Cox International — 6.25% $ 62,465
- PIMCO Foreign Bond (US Dollar Hedg) — 4.95% $ 49,458

Other Products 12.50% $ 124,967

Legend:
- High Yield Bonds
- Small Growth Stocks
- International Stocks
- Large Value Stocks
- MidCap Stocks
- International Bonds
- Large Growth Stocks
- Real Estate
- Emerging Equities
- Small Value Stocks
- Futures/Commodities

Table 47 shows the suggested changes in the qualified assets in the proposed asset allocation plan. Small differences in the dollar amounts may be due to rounding.

Table 47. Plan Implementation.

Implementation Plan - Uses of Qualified Assets

Proposed Asset Class	Investment Recommendation	Symbol	Proposed $	Proposed %	Source of Funds
High Yield Bonds	Amer Funds Hi Inc Trst F	AHTFX	$ 92,711	9.27%	Vanguard 500 Index
Large Value Stocks	Amer Funds Wash Mutual F	WSHFX	$ 49,965	5.00%	Vanguard 500 Index
	DWS Dreman High Return	KDHAX	50,000	5.00	Vanguard 500 Index
	Pioneer Cullen Value A	CVFCX	50,000	5.00	Vanguard 500 Index
			$ 149,966	15.00%	
Large Growth Stocks	Amer Funds Amcap F	AMPFX	$ 50,000	5.00%	Vanguard 500 Index
	Amer Funds Grth Fnd F	GFAFX	49,965	5.00	Vanguard 500 Index
	Marsico 21 Cent Grth	NMTAX	50,000	5.00	Vanguard 500 Index
			$ 149,966	15.00%	
Small Value Stocks	DWS Dreman Small Value	KDSAX	$ 57,821	5.78%	Vanguard 500 Index
Small Growth Stocks	Amer Funds Small Wld F	SCWFX	$ 50,243	5.02%	Vanguard 500 Index
MidCap Stocks	RS Mid Cap Value	RSVAX	$ 50,000	5.00%	Vanguard 500 Index
	Security Mid Cap Value	SEVAX	49,967	5.00	Vanguard 500 Index
			$ 99,967	10.00%	
Real Estate	Cohen & Steers Global Real Estate Fund	CSFAX	$ 49,968	5.00%	Vanguard 500 Index
Futures/Commodities	DWS Commodity Fund	SKNRX	$ 49,968	5.00%	Vanguard 500 Index
International Stocks	Amer Funds Euro Pacific F	AEGFX	$ 62,500	6.25%	Vanguard 500 Index
	Dodge and Cox International	DODFX	62,465	6.25	Vanguard 500 Index
	DWS Japan	FJEAX	25,000	2.50	Vanguard 500 Index
			$ 149,966	15.00%	
International Bonds	PIMCO Foreign Bond (US Dollar Hedged)	PFOAX	$ 49,458	4.95%	Vanguard 500 Index
Emerging Equities	AIM China	AACFX	$ 33,000	3.30%	Vanguard 500 Index
	Amer Funds New World F	NWFFX	33,000	3.30	Vanguard 500 Index
	Eastern European Equity	VEEEX	33,967	3.40	Vanguard 500 Index

Implementation Plan - Uses of Qualified Assets

Proposed Asset Class	Investment Recommendation	Symbol	Proposed $	Proposed %	Source of Funds
			$ 99,967	10.00%	
Total Qualified Assets			$ 1,000,000		

10. Goals and Constraints

In addition to individual portfolio risk and financial market data, goals and constraints may also be needed to select or optimize a portfolio. Constraints might be used to constrain the optimizer solution.

Goals

Goals should be dollar and date specific. One conservative rule of thumb is that investments with a time frame less than 5 years should not be in the market. This is because one bull-bear market cycle (business, or presidential cycle) is roughly 5 years.

Goals: *date*

3-12 months cash reserves needed are $_____   _____

Rainy day reserve needs: $_____ for _____ months of living expenses   _____
Disability insurance needs: $_____ for _____ months of disability   _____
Life insurance needs: $_____ for _____ years of income   _____

College education funds needed for:

Child _____ $_____ for _____ college for _____ years   _____

Wedding expenses needed for:

Child _____ $_____   _____

Retirement money: Income from investments _____ /year to live on   _____

Other needs $_____   _____

Constraints

For each goal, list dollar amount needed, tax situation, risk tolerance, and resources to be used. For example:

Goal	No. of years	$ needed	Investment resource < 5 years?
Emergency reserve	4 mo living expenses	4 x mo. budget	no
Daughter wedding	1 year	$20,000	no
Retirement	20 years	20 yrs x .8 x $120,000 = $1,920,000	yes

11. Example Investment Policy Statement

An investment policy statement provides formal financial goals. An example of an investment policy statement is given below. (Source: adapted from Gardner, J. *How to Write an Investment Policy Statement*, 2003, Market Place Books). A policy statement can guide the *Jackson family trust* and it's investment advisor in supervising, monitoring, and evaluating the investments.

The *Jackson family trust* desires to obtain a yearly return from ____ to ____ within a level of risk from ___ to ____ to meet the following investment objectives: _____.

The minimum expected investment period is: _____ years. For less time than 4 years the investment shall be in bonds.

The *Jackson family trust* has retained The **Wealth Manager** of _____ firm to manage the wealth management process through several specialists including investment manager(s), estate lawyer(s), insurance specialist(s), etc. The Wealth Manager is a generalist who does not own the investment return and risk. The primary responsibilities of the wealth manager include:

- Prepare statement of investment objectives
- Provide return and risk guidelines
- Select, monitor, and supervise investment managers
- Act in a fiduciary role by avoiding conflicts of interest and prohibited transactions and put client interest first.

The wealth manager will select and monitoring each investment manager or mutual fund manager such that:

- Investment manager(s) should be in place for at least five years
- The manager, mutual fund, or hedge fund fees should be reasonable and representative. Common buy-and-hold management should charge less than 1% per year. Active management should charge less than 3% per year
- Hidden and back end commissions including 12(b)-1 should be understood and acceptable.

The Investment/Money Manager(s) is (are) responsible for making investments in areas including: mutual funds, ETFs, stocks, bonds, third party money managers, hedge fund managers, etc. The Investment Manager is a specialist who owns the investment return and risk. The duties and responsibilities of each investment manager include:

- Manage assets in the *Jackson family trust* according to formal guidelines and objectives.
- Vote or not vote all proxies. Maintain records and comply with regulatory rules.
- Report on significant gains/losses in dollars managed
- Obtain "best price and execution". Report all "soft dollar" arrangements to trustees
- Manage according to all applicable laws, rules, and regulations.

The custodian safeguards the *Jackson family trust* portfolio assets by:

- Providing monthly report of transactions, cash flows, and security values

- Maintaining separate registration accounts
- Collecting income and dividends
- Settling all buy-sell orders.

Periodically, the *Jackson family trust* Wealth Manager will meet with the trustee(s) to review each investment manager's progress in areas such as:

- Adherence to the formal investment guidelines
- Anticipate withdrawals and disbursements and notify investment managers as needed
- Current holding consistent with the investment strategy and guidelines
- Compare performance to relevant benchmarks
- Evidence that the investment managers are seeking "best execution" and avoiding soft dollar problems.
- Material changes in investment manager's organization, investment philosophy, and personnel
- SEC, or state regulatory agency proceedings affecting the investment manager

Sample Investment Policy/Financial Plan Summary
Jackson family trust

October 2007

Type of assets	Personal and 401(k)
Current Assets	$2.35 million
Investment Time Horizon	Greater than 7 years
Expected Return	CPI plus 5%
Risk Tolerance	Aggressive growth
Losses less than 12% per year	

Fixed Asset Allocation	cash	2%
	U.S. bonds	5
	International bonds	8
	U.S. Large cap	25
	U.S. Small cap	25
	International	25
	Commercial REIT	10
Allocation standard deviation limit	quarterly	14
Broad classes	yearly	7
Representative benchmarks	cash	Donoghue Tax MMA
	Fixed income	Lehman aggregate
	Equity	S&P500
	Growth & Income	
	MSCI	
	Growth	
	Small Com	
	International	
	EAFE	

Table 48 shows the asset allocation for the *Jackson Family Trust*.

Table 48. Example of Asset Allocation Policy for Fixed Income, $1. Million and Equity $1.3 Million.

Investment T-bills & note policy allocation: $1,000,000.

Intermediate muni bonds	$131,000
Intermediate bonds	156,000
Money market	13,000
Short term corp/Govt	165,000
Short Intermediate Govt/corp	178,000
Short muni bonds	135,000
Short intermediate muni bonds	222,000

Investment equity policy allocation: $1,265,000.

Commercial REIT	$166,000
Emerging markets	132,000
Europe	132,000
Large cap blend	145,000
Large cap growth	155,000
Large cap value	190,000
Small cap growth	177,000
Small cap value	168,000

Typical Plan Passive Allocations

Many passive investment managers select a reference index, allocate very close to its values, and hope to obtain similar return and risk. Passive managers usually have a low portfolio turnover of less than 30%. Manager might change allocation weights by + -10% from reference weights. An example of the MSCI index with sector and country weights is provided in Table 49.

Table 49. Example of MSCI World Index Weights.
(Source: Thompson Financial Datastream, June 30, 2006).

Sector	Weight
Financials	25.6
Consumer discretionary	11.2
Industrials	10.8
Information technology	10.4
Energy	9.9
Health care	9.6
Consumer staples	8.0
Materials	6.1
Telecommunication services	4.2
Utilities	4.1
Total	100.0%

Country	weight
USA	49.5%
Japan	11.5
United Kingdom	11.3
France	4.6
Canada	3.8
Germany	3.3
Switzerland	3.2
Austria	2.5
Spain	1.8
Total	100.

12. Annotated Bibliography

Published academic investment literature is briefly reviewed here. The articles form a baseline of technology employed by the buy-and-hold financial community. The literature is generally based on the mean variance teaching, begun in 1952, that good portfolios are diversified and that optimal asset allocations can be determined by constrained or unconstrained computer optimization. The assumptions are that investing is a steady-state process and that the input numbers, needed for the math optimization, are constants.

However, real life investing is not constant, buy-and-hold is not ideal, and other active strategies methods are available. Before reviewing the literature, there are a few investing concepts that are outside the "buy-and-hold a diversified portfolio cannon". For example:

1. Warren Buffet teaches us that one can obtain superior results by: taking a very long-term view (buy-and-hold), concentrating the top 5 holdings to be 70% of the portfolio, and buying large cap growth when company prices are low (buy value large cap growth).
2. Active money management as practiced by hedge funds is considered a new asset class to the buy-and-hold community. Thus, the new active asset class has the same "overlay" of diversification and fixed allocation weights as other investment. Some professionals believe that active investing management is fundamentally different than buy-and-hold management and is a viable competitor for the management of entire portfolios.

a. Private Wealth Management: Goals and Constraints

Brinson, Hood, and Beebower, "Determinants of Portfolio Performance", Financial Analyst Journal 1986, 39-44.
Ten years of data from 91 large U.S. pension plans from 1974 to 1983 are examined to determine relative performance attributes. No employee designated plans are included. Returns on the passive "investment policy" portfolio are compared to actual returns where: (a) active changes are made to the asset classes relative to the plan benchmark (called market timing), and (b) security selection (or mutual fund manager) within an asset class. The study has a shortcoming in that the 10-year mean average holding of each asset class are used as a proxy for the unknown actual asset allocation plan. Thus the study compares not actual plan asset class weights, but 10-year average returns weights. In other words the study is based on average and not actual policy weights.

Average holdings are listed below in Table 50. Common stock, bonds plus cash, and other are 57.5%, 33.8%, and 8.6% respectively.

Table 50. Summary Holdings of 91 Large Pension Plans, 1974-1983.
(Source: Brinson, G.P., Hood, L.R., and Beebower, G.L.,"Determinant of Portfolio Performance", Financial Analyst Journal, July-August 1986, 39-44).

Table IV Summary of Holdings of 91 Large Pension Plans, 1974-1983

All Holdings	Average	Minimum	Maximum	Standard Deviation	Policy Benchmark
Common Stock	57.5%	32.3%	86.5%	10.9%	S&P 500 Total Return Index (S&P 500)
Bonds	21.4	0.0	43.0	9.0	Shearson Lehman Government/Corporate Bond Index (SLGC)
Cash Equivalents	12.4	1.8	33.1	5.0	30-Day Treasury Bills
Other	8.6	0.0	53.5	8.3	None
	100.0%				
Stocks, Bonds and Cash Only					
Common Stock	62.9%	37.9%	89.3%	10.6%	
Bonds	23.4	0.0	51.3	9.4	
Cash Equivalents	13.6	2.0	35.0	5.2	
	100.0%				

Table 51 indicates that the 10-year average "actual" portfolio earns 9.01 % (with a wide variation from 5.85% to 13.4%), the policy and selection portfolio earns 9.75% (from 7.17% to 13.31%), and the policy and timing portfolio earns 9.44% (from 7.25% to 13.31%). The 10-year average "policy" portfolio return is 10.11%.

Table 51. Annualized 10-Year Returns of Large Plans, 1974-1983.
(Source: Brinson, G.P., Hood, L.R., and Beebower, G.L.,"Determinant of Portfolio Performance", Financial Analyst Journal, July-August 1986, 39-44).

Table VI Annualized 10-Year Returns of 91 Large Plans, 1974-1983

Portfolio Total Returns	Average Return	Minimum Return	Maximum Return	Standard Deviation
Policy	10.11%	9.47%	10.57%	0.22%
Policy and Timing	9.44	7.25	10.34	0.52
Policy and Selection	9.75	7.17	13.31	1.33
Actual Portfolio	9.01	5.85	13.40	1.43
Active Returns				
Timing Only	-0.66%	-2.68%	0.25%	0.49%
Security Selection Only	-0.36	-2.90	3.60	1.36
Other	-0.07	-1.17	2.57	0.45
Total Active Return	-1.10%	-4.17%*	3.69%*	1.45%*

The regression goodness of fit is known as R^2 and can be said to equal the % of variance explained by the curve fit. Table 52 indicates that the equations employed explain from 93% to 98 % of the variance. The difference in R^2 between 93.6% and 97.8% is fairly small at about 4.5%. The "variance explained" result has been widely misunderstood in the financial literature with many financial professionals incorrectly thinking that Policy accounts for 93.6% of return.

The standard deviation is 2.9% for "Policy and Timing", 3.1% for Policy and Selection, and 4.4% for Policy. The difference between these standard deviations is 52%. The lower standard deviation for Policy and Timing indicates to Harloff, that "Policy and Timing" (market timing) is a lower risk policy than "Policy and Selection".

This study is updated and is included below under section Asset Allocation for Private Investors.

Table 52. Goodness of Fit Explained from Brinson et. al. 1986.
(Source: Brinson, G.P., Hood, L.R., and Beebower, G.L.,"Determinant of Portfolio Performance", Financial Analyst Journal, July-August 1986, 39-44).

	\multicolumn{3}{c}{Variance Explained}		
	Average	Minimum	Maximum	Standard Deviation
Policy	93.6%	75.5%	98.6%	4.4%
Policy and Timing	95.3	78.7	98.7	2.9
Policy and Selection	97.8	80.6	99.8	3.1

Jeffrey and Arnott, "Is your Alpha Big Enough to Cover Its Taxes?", The Journal of Portfolio Management, 1993, 15-25.
Jeffrey and Arnott discuss the detrimental effects of realized capital gains taxes on total return. They examine 72 large equity mutual funds from 1982 through 1991 and show the funds after-tax growth. They argue that avoiding realizing capital gains in taxable equity portfolios preserves long-term wealth. Of the 71 equity mutual funds with over $100 million in assets, only 15 beat the S&P500 on a pretax basis, and only 6 after taxes. They also show that 8.2% pre-tax growth is needed to equal a 5 % growth rate at 5% annual turnover. Higher than 100% turnover rates add only a little to the needed pre-tax growth rate as the curve levels off around this rate.

Applebach, R.O., Jr., "The Capital Gains Tax Penalty", Journal of Portfolio Management, (Summer) 1995, pp. 99-103.
Applebach discusses the issue that high-net worth clients will not recognize capital gains to improve portfolio diversification. He compares the risk/return for selling low-cost-basis stocks and paying capital gains taxes to the buy-and-hold risk/return profiles. He concludes that holding low-cost-basis stocks to avoid paying capital gains taxes may not always be prudent. And, selling a portion of these stocks can reduce risk and enhance capital preservation.

Applebach looks at the HNW individual's propensity of not recognizing capital gains to improve portfolio diversification. This may be partly due to the assets receiving a "step-up" basis upon death transfer. There are opportunity costs of holding non-optimal portfolios. The article measures 15-year return and risk for buy-and-hold and compares this to portfolio results where low-cost-stocks are sold, capital gains tax paid, and reinvesting after tax proceeds into a fully diversified portfolio. The 9 hypothetical stocks are selected randomly and combined with 10% invested in Treasury bills. Seven 15-year periods are analyzed from June 1972 through June 1987 and ending in June 1978 through June 1993. Modified portfolios are formed by selling 20 % of the original stocks in the buy-and-hold portfolio, over a 5-year period starting at the end of the 7th year (of 15), and invested in the S&P500 index. The return and risk are illustrated in Figure 23 and may be representative of the variation of return and risk obtained in real life. The selling strategy reduces, compared to buy-and-hold, the standard deviation risk for all seven 15-year periods examined. The average return is not significantly lower for four of the seven cases, than buy-and-hold.

EXHIBIT 4
FIFTEEN-YEAR ANNUAL COMPOUNDED RETURN AND RISK FOR THE PERIOD ENDING JUNE 30, 1993

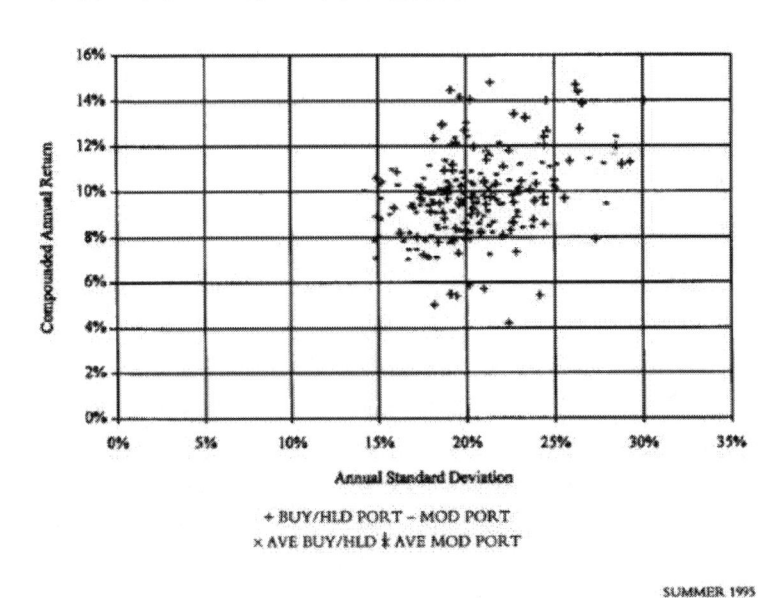

(Source: Applebach, R.O., Jr. "The Capital Gains Tax Penalty", Journal of Portfolio Management, (Summer) 1995, 99-103).

Figure 23. Fifteen-Year Annual Compounded Return and Risk for the Period Ending June 30, 1993.

Arnott, R.D., Berkin, A.L., and Ye, J., "How Well Have Taxable Investors Been Served in the 1980s and 1990s"?, Journal of Portfolio Management, vol. 20, no. 4, (Summer) 2000, 84-93.
This paper examines post tax return for all $100 million mutual funds in 1979, 1984, and 1989. They conclude that over the last 20 years only 14% outperform the Vanguard 500 index on a pretax basis. The average mutual fund under performed the index by 1.75% pretax, 2.58% after capital gains and dividend taxation, and 2.00 % after all taxes.

b. Risk Evaluation of Private Investors

Sharpe, W. F., Goldstein, D. G., and Blythe, P.W., "The Distribution Builder: A Tool for Inferring Investor Preferences, Working Paper", Stanford University 2000, <*http://www.stanford.edu/~wfsharpe/art/qpaper/qpaper.html*>.
This paper describes an interactive tool to determine investor's preferences to eventually lead to more accurate equilibrium investment models. The capital asset pricing model assumes the investor wishes to maximize a linear function of mean and variance of portfolio return. This leads to more stocks for investors with high-risk tolerance and more bonds for investors with less risk tolerance.

Kapteyn, A. and Teppa, F., "Subjective Measures of Risk Aversion and Portfolio Choice", No. 2002-11, ISSN 0924-7815, CentER, Amsterdam February 2002.
This paper investigates different methods used to measure risk preferences for eventual use in portfolio asset allocation. They conclude that risk tolerance has little explanatory power. Simple intuitive risk preference measures may be more useful than more complex measures.

c. Private Wealth Management and Modern Investment Theory

Bodie, Z., "On the Risk of Stocks in the Long Run", Financial Analysts Journal, 1995, 51, 18-22.
This paper concludes that one commonly held belief is wrong. Namely, that younger people should invest in more stocks because they have a longer investment time horizon, and older people should invest more in bonds because they have a shorter investment time horizon. One measure of risk is shortfall, i.e. the difference between a portfolio value at a future time and a target value. Bodie argues that if the above proposition is correct, then the cost of insuring against earning less than the risk-free (zero coupon bonds maturing at the horizon date) rate of interest should decline as investment horizon lengthens. But the opposite case occurs. He employs (European) put option theory to price insurance. He concludes that inflation adjusted bonds provide an inflation hedge whereas stocks are uncorrelated with inflation and are not long-term "real" bonds.

Thorley, S.R., "The Time Diversification Controversy", Financial Analysts Journal, May-June 1995, 51, 68-76.
Thorley addresses how investment time horizon affects risk aversion. Most practitioners would say that young investors should allocate more to stocks than older investors. Thorley indicates that some financial models are inadequate given that investors rightly divine that stocks return more than bonds over the long run.

Fogler, H.R., "Investment Analysis and New Quantitative Tools", Journal of Portfolio Management, (Summer) 1995, 39-48.
Fogler shows that Russell growth stock returns explain 57% of value stocks returns (i.e. correlation or R^2 is 0.57). He suggests that profitable quantitative investment software won't be commercialized because if it were, then prices would incorporate this information.

d. Asset Allocation for Private Investors

DeMiguel, V., Garlappi, L., Uppal, R. "How Inefficient are Simple Asset-Allocation Strategies?", October 25, 2004 and March 2005. <www.newton.cam.ac.uk/webseminars/pg+ws/2005/dqf/0314/uppal/all.pdf>.
This paper finds that 1/n weighting of n assets available produces a higher Sharpe ratio and lower turnover than policies from static optimal asset-allocation strategies.

Brinson, G.P., Singer, B.D., and Beebower, G.L., "Determinants of Portfolio Performance II: An Update", Financial Analyst Journal 1991, 40-48.
This paper follows the 1986 Brinson, G.P., Hood, L.R., Beebower, G.L. study with a new similar study with 82 large pension plans from 1977-1987 and finds that equations explain 91.5 % of the variation in quarterly plan total returns. Asset allocation policy is the setting of normal asset class weights as specified in the investment policy. Active asset allocation is the relative changing of these weights over time, to the nominal policy weights. The average weights, excluding the unknown "other category" over the decade are: 59.6% equity, 26.9% bonds, 13.6% cash. A 60/40 stock/bond asset allocation performs about as good as the average return. The "other category" might have been real estate since it is usually a low volatility investment. On an equity basis, 93% or 76 of the 82 equity pension plans under performed the S&P500 index. Figure 24shows the wide variation in bond weights, from 5 to 53%, compared to equity weights in the data analyzed. Active asset allocation (market timing or small weight changing from the investment plan) gave about the same answer, as did security selection in terms of the average returns. The authors' conclusion is that it is hard for active management to beat index portfolio returns; only about 7% beat the S&P500 index.

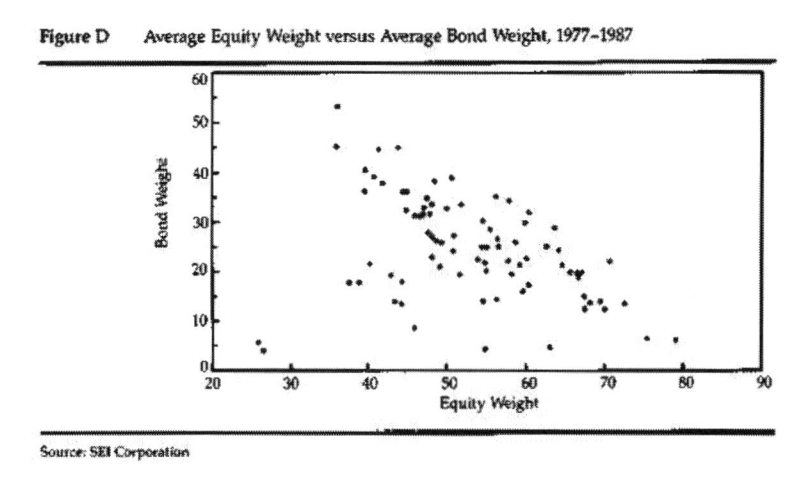

Figure D Average Equity Weight versus Average Bond Weight, 1977-1987

Source: SEI Corporation

FINANCIAL ANALYSTS JOURNAL / MAY-JUNE 1991 □ 43

(Source: Brinson, G.P., Singer, B.D., and Beebower G.L., "Determinants of Portfolio Performance II: An Update", Financial Analyst Journal 1991, 40-48).

Figure 24. Average Equity Weight vs. Average Bond Weight, 1977-1987.

Pension plan return vs. risk is quite variable as indicated below in Figure 25

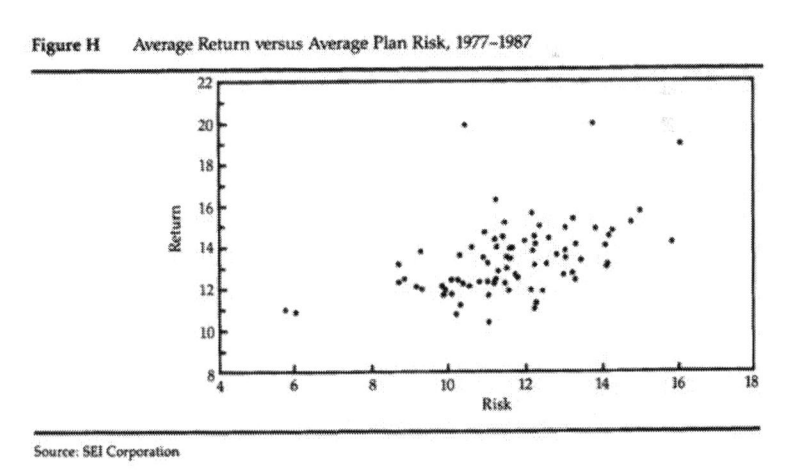

Figure H Average Return versus Average Plan Risk, 1977-1987

Source: SEI Corporation

(Source: Brinson, G.P., Singer, B.D., and Beebower G.L., "Determinants of Portfolio Performance II: An Update", Financial Analyst Journal 1991, 40-48).

Figure 25. Average Return vs. Average Plan Risk, 1977-1987.

Hensel, C.R., Ezra, D.D., and Ilkiw, J.H., "The Importance of the Asset Allocation Decision", Financial Analysts Journal 1991, 65-72.
This paper discusses the importance of asset allocation. It is widely though that the investor asset allocation policy statement is more important than small changes in allocation (market timing) or security selection. This paper examines 7 retirement plans from 1985 to 1988 for different types of decisions on both return and return variability. The average quarterly total fund return is 3.86%. This is comprised of: T-bills accounting for 1.62%, policy allocation accounts for 2.13%, specific policy allocation accounts for 0.49%, active management costs 0.10%, security selection costs 0.23%, and the interaction of timing and stock selection costs 0.05%.

Michaud, R.O., "The Markowitz Optimization Enigma: Is Optimized Optimal?" Financial Analysts Journal, January-February 1989, 31-41.
Problems with practical application of the Markowitz mean-variance procedure are discussed. Michaud argues that the application of an optimizer may magnify input error estimates and provide optimal asset allocation weights that are less useful than equal weights. Adding client investment consideration constraints on sector and industry solution allocation weights may be useful.

Carhart, M.M., "Global Tactical Asset Allocation", Modern Investment Management, Goldman Sachs Asset Management, 2003, 455-482.
The goal of this strategy is to increase return per unit risk by active management of asset allocation deviations, or market timing. A brief history recalls that Charles Dow, founder of the Wall Street Journal, was a great market timer, while Benjamin Graham was a skeptic. William Fouse in the early 1970's developed a tactical asset allocation strategy in response to the 1973-1974 bear market, and stock index and bond future markets provided a low cost means to implement it. Global Tactical Asset Allocation (TAA) strategies were developed in the late 1980 and early 1990's with the improvement in global market liquidity. The Fed model, that relates P/E to 10-year yields can be used to compute an earnings gap. A model based on these numbers shows that $1. in 1928 grows to $3.30 by 2001 as illustrated in Figure 26. There are about 25 investment firms

globally that offer TAA/GTAA services. These managers have: a sound investment philosophy based on theoretical and empirical evidence, a quantitative approach, active strategies across strategies, themes, a risk budget, an independent risk management group, and continued stock market research.

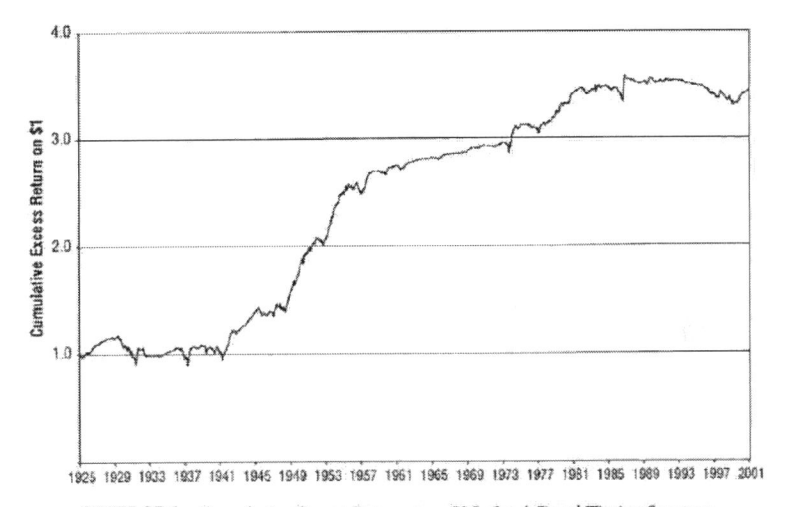

FIGURE 25.1 Cumulative Excess Return on a U.S. Stock/Bond Timing Strategy

(Source:Carhart, M.M., "Global Tactical Asset Allocation", Modern Investment Management, Goldman Sachs Asset Management, 2003, 455-482).

Figure 26. Cumulative Excess Return on a U.S. Stock/Bond Timing Strategy.

Leibowitz, M.L., and Hammond, P.B., "The Changing Mosaic of Investment Patterns", Journal of Portfolio Management, Spring 2004, vol. 30, n0. 3, 10-25.
This paper asks these questions: (1) how do different investors respond to equity movements, (2) how do we understand these behaviors, and (3) what are the implications for equity markets?

Individual asset allocation patterns for all TIAA-CREF defined-contributions pension non-retired participants are shown in Figure 27. Cash and money market account for 5%. Fixed income and equity vary slowly with time. From the end of 1994 equity allocations went from 48% to 65% in 1999.

The fact that asset allocation changes over time is inconsistent with the buy-and-hold strategy.

EXHIBIT 2
Individual Pension Asset Allocation—TIAA-CREF Premium Paying and Paid-Up Participants

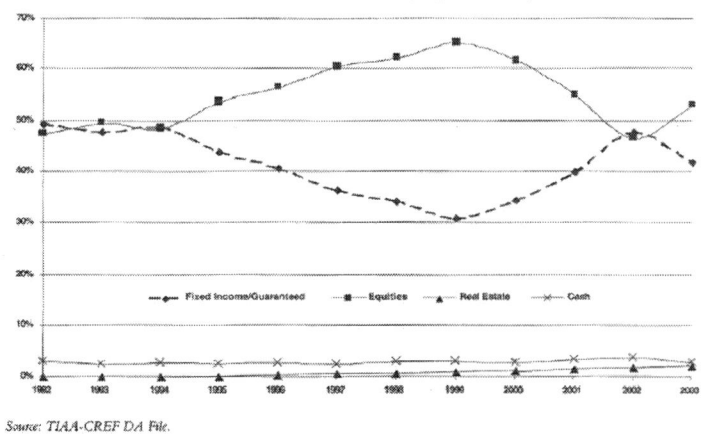

Source: TIAA-CREF DA File.

(Source: Leibowitz, M.L., and Hammond, P.B., "The Changing Mosaic of Investment Patterns", Journal of Portfolio Management, Spring 2004, vol. 30, n0. 3, 10-25).

Figure 27. Pension Asset Allocation—TIAA-CREF Premium Paying and Paid-Up Participants.

Similar asset allocations over time are illustrated in Figure 28 for college/university endowments and show a peak of about 65% equity in 1999. This trend is very similar to the individual pension allocation in Figure 27

EXHIBIT 3

College/University Endowment Asset Allocation

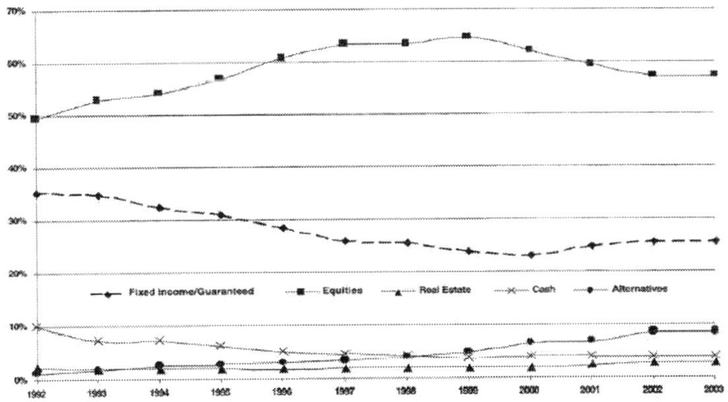

Source: NACUBO College and University Endowment Survey conducted by TIAA-CREF and Cambridge Associates.

(Source: Leibowitz, M.L., and Hammond, P.B., "The Changing Mosaic of Investment Patterns", Journal of Portfolio Management, Spring 2004, vol. 30, n0. 3, 10-25).

Figure 28. College/University Endowment Asset Allocation.

Average asset allocation in 2003 for college/university endowment funds generally have 69-74% stock and 26 to 33% bonds, see Table 53.

Table 53. College/University Endowments: 2003 Average Asset Allocation.
(Source: Leibowitz, M.L., and Hammond, P.B., "The Changing Mosaic of Investment Patterns", Journal of Portfolio Management, Spring 2004, vol. 30, n0. 3, 10-25.)

EXHIBIT 4

College/University Endowments—2003 Average Asset Allocation

	All Asset Classes			Equity/Fixed Only	
$ Endowment Assets	Equity	Fixed-Income	Alternatives	Equity	Fixed-Income
Greater than 1.0 Billion	45	20	32	69	31
500 Million-1.0 Billion	56	20	22	74	26
100 Million-500 Million	57	25	13	69	31
Less than 100 Million	59	29	6	67	33
Total	56	25	14	69	31

Source: NACUBO College and University Endowment Survey conducted by TIAA-CREF and Cambridge Associates.

Endowment and individual pension equity allocation, considering only equity and bonds, both change over time and individuals tend to be about 10 to 18% more conservative than endowments, see Figure 29. Endowments are probably more aggressive than individuals because the endowments have professional portfolio management.

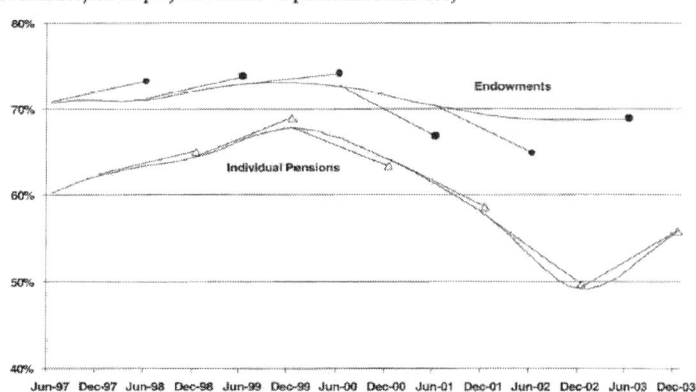

EXHIBIT 5
Actual versus Projected Equity Allocations—Equities and Bonds Only

Source: Individual Pensions (TIAA-CREF), College Endowments (NACUBO Survey, TIAA-CREF).

(Source: Leibowitz, M.L., and Hammond, P.B., "The Changing Mosaic of Investment Patterns", Journal of Portfolio Management, Spring 2004, vol. 30, n0. 3, 10-25).

Figure 29. Annual vs. Projected Equity Allocations—Equities and Bonds Only.

e. Tax Investing Issues

Wilcox, J., Horvitz, J., DiBartolomeo, D., Investment Management for Taxable Private Investors, Research Foundation of CFA Institute, 2006.

High taxes reduce investment wealth return, but high return trumps low return. As shown in Table 54 with an initial investment of $10,000, after a 20-year investment period, a 5% growth rate, and a 15% tax rate returns $12,990. By comparison, a 10% growth rate and a 35% tax rate return $25,240. Thus, many conservative investors who covet low tax rates may be penny wise and pound-foolish.

Table 54. Additional Wealth From $10,000 Invested After Different Return and Tax Rates Applied.
(Source: Wilcox, J., Horvitz, J., diBartolomeo, D., Investment Management for Taxable Private Investors, Research Foundation of CFA Institute, 2006).

Table 6.1. Additional Wealth from $10,000 Invested after Different Return and Tax Rates Applied

Return and Tax	5 Years	10 Years	20 Years
Rate of return = 5%			
15% LTCG tax	$2,310	$ 5,160	$12,990
35% STCG tax	1,730	3,770	8,960
Rate of return = 10%			
15% LTCG tax	$5,040	$12,610	$41,120
35% STCG tax	3,700	8,770	25,240

Notes: LTCG = long-term capital gains; STCG = short-term capital gains.

13. Summary and Conclusions

Wealth management for individuals, universities, and family offices is largely conducted in the same way. Modern portfolio theory started in 1952 and is still the primary method used to allocate portfolios. This is a passive investment technique with long-term statistics input to the optimization computer programs. Because computer power has increased over the last 20 years, the optimizer computer programs are pervasive and enable individual financial professionals to provide potential clients with sophisticated looking proposals. The limitations of this mathematical process are not widely understood by most financial professionals at the wealth manager/financial planner level. To see the limitations one only has to ask if the MPT projected returns were achieved during the 2000 to 2003 bear market.

It is not uncommon for mean-variance optimized, buy-and-hold until next year, portfolios to return single digit returns, and return less than S&P500 returns. Other, more actively managed, portfolios typically stay close to a target index and may provide returns close to the reference index. In contrast to the norm, Warren Buffet earned almost 2 times the S&P500 return by buying cheap, concentrating his investments in a single style box (currently large cap growth), and rarely selling.

Many wealth managers inappropriately wear two hats: one as a wealth manager/coach and another hat as an investment manager. The wealth manager is a generalist and the investment manager is a specialist. One or the other must own the investment result and be held accountable for performance.

The academic literature seems to support the static allocation-over-diversified-buy-and-hold-check-back-next year strategy. This is understandable due to the nature of academic research and research papers. Most of the literature is about *employing* MPT and *comparing* portfolio returns and volatility with other portfolios that are also managed with MPT. Academic journal gate keepers are limiting contributions of active portfolio management. It is straightforward for academics to analyze historic portfolio returns with the MPT governing process. In contrast, it is not easy to evaluate active management results because the active strategies are not the same. There are not yet any equations of motion (governing differential equations) that describes the investing process that can be scientifically studied. This state of the investing process is in contrast to scientific fields with well-defined processes such as physics, computational fluid dynamics, mechanical engineering, and aerospace engineering.

The recent popularity of hedge funds is embraced by academics as an asset class. But active investing is not yet embraced as a stand-alone method of managing entire endowment and pension portfolios. One attraction of pooled hedge funds is they offer inherently low correlation returns to the S&P500 index. This feature is a result of an active investing process in both long and short positions.

The mutual funds currently dominate the investing landscape and it is in their best interest to prevent money from leaving their fund family. Thus, it is easy to see why most mutual funds promote a buy-and-hold approach. Over time, the new investment vehicles of ETFs will diminish the importance of the mutual fund's buy-and-hold/redemption fee approach.

The literature indicates that the endowment and individual pension funds stock/bond ratio changes slowly. This changing ratio is at odds with the static once-for-all-time asset allocation strategy that is one of the pillars of mean variance optimization. One explanation for this behavior is that the statistical inputs into MPT computer programs may be changing slowly. However, many practitioners of MPT employ statistics based on up to 30 years of data.

Market timing, or tactical/dynamic asset allocation, offers an alternate strategy to buy-and-hold but has not yet reached an equivalent level of description as modern portfolio theory. Until it does, the sales force can't replicate it, and it will remain in the realm of boutique registered investment advisor companies and hedge funds.

14. Appendix. Outline of Wealth Management Body of Knowledge

An outline of wealth management body of knowledge from the CFA Institute is included here for completeness. The listing illustrates the general body of knowledge of CFA exam-pass designated individuals. (Source: <https://www.cfainstitute.org/memresources/pdf/pwm_bok.pdf—Source: draft>).

I. Ethics
A. Standards, ethics, and regulations (SER)
B. Fiduciary duty
C. Advocacy
D. Professional development and competence improvement

II. The Private Client Marketplace and Firm Management
A. Global trends in wealth management and private banking
B. Collaboration and investment teams
C. Employee management and remuneration
D. Service delivery platforms
E. Institutions serving the private client
F. Communicating with a team of professionals
G. Attracting and retaining desirable clients

III. Analysis of the Client
A. Relationship management
B. Fact gathering and analysis
C. Application of Behavioral Finance to Wealth Management
D. Analysis of Investor Psychology
E. Risk Tolerance
F. Investment objectives and horizons

IV. Wealth Management Planning and Instruments
A. Wealth Management Process
B. Asset protection and risk management
C. Income Tax Planning
D. Education Planning
E. Retirement Planning and Employee Benefits
F. Wealth Transfer
G. Investment Policy Statement (IPS)
H. Developing a wealth management plan

V. Portfolio Management for Taxable Investors
A. Asset allocation for the taxable investor
B. Portfolio construction and strategy
C. Implementation
D. Monitoring and rebalancing
E. Performance evaluation

15. References

A to Z Investments, <*http://www.atozinvestments.com/mutual-fund-index.html*>.

Applebach, R.O., Jr., "The Capital Gains Tax Penalty", The Journal of Portfolio Management, (Summer) 1995, 99-103.

Arnott, R.D., Berkin, A.L., and Ye, J. "How Well Have Taxable Investors Been Served in the 1980s and 1990s?", Journal of Portfolio Management, vol. 20, no. 4, (Summer) 2000, 84-93.

Barrons, October 22, 2007, 34.

Bodie, Z., "On the Risk of Stocks in the Long Run", Financial Analysts Journal, May-June 1995, 51, 18-22.

Boston Consulting Group, Reported by Barrons, October 22, 2007, 34.

Brinson, G.P., Hood, L.R., and Beebower, G.L. "Determinants of Portfolio Performance," Financial Analyst Journal, July-August 1986, 39-44.

Brinson, G.P., Singer, B.D., and Beebower, G.L., "Determinants of Portfolio Performance II: An Update", Financial Analyst Journal 1991, 40-48.

Callan, "Annual Returns for Key Indices" (1987-2006), <*http://www.callan.com/resource/*>.

Canadian Institute of Financial Planners, September 2006. <*www.advisor.ca/practice/running_your_business/article.jsp?content=20060912_113157_=1560*>.

Carhart, M.M., "Global Tactical Asset Allocation", Modern Investment Management, Goldman Sachs Asset Management, 2003, 455-482.

CFA Institute, <*www.cfawebcasts.org*>.

CFA Institute, "Outline of Wealth Management Body of Knowledge", <https://www.cfainstitute.org/memresources/pdf/pwm_bok.pdf>.

Charter Financial Publishing Network, "Cultivating the Affluent Newsletter", October 2007.

Dalbar Inc., Boston, MA, "Quantitative Analysis of Investor Behavior Study", 1997, 1998, 2000, 2003, 2008, 2009 Updates; for example: (1984-2002) <http://www.dalbarinc.com/contents/showpage.asp?page=2003071601&r=/pressroom/defa> . . . accessed 10/21/2004, (1988-2007) <http://www.slideshare.net/dkeogh/3919Davis-Advisors-The-Wisdom-of-Great-Investors-

Module-Presentation-0608-3919-834467> p 4, (1998-2008) *http://www.scribd.com/doc/13096471/DALBAR-QAIB-2008.*

DeMiguel, V., Garlappi, L., Uppal, R., "How Inefficient are Simple Asset-Allocation Strategies?" October 25, 2004 and March 2005.

Federal Reserve Board, "Survey of Consumer Finances", 2001.

Fogler, H.R., "Investment Analysis and New Quantitative Tools", Journal of Portfolio Management (Summer) 1995, 39-48.

Gardner, J., How to Write an Investment Policy Statement, Market Place Books, 2003.

Gibson, R., IAFP Advanced Planner Conference, 1992.

Glenmede, Private Wealth Management Summit, San Juan Puerto Rico, April 18-20, 2002.

Goyal, A., "Course Notes", HEC Lausanne: Master of Science in Finance, Investments, Fall. 2007, <*https://www.hec.unil.ch/docs/agoyal/04.portfolio_optimization[1].ppt*>.

Goyal, A., "Course Notes", HEC Lausanne: Master of Science in Finance, Investments, Fall 2007, <*https://www.hec.unil.ch/docs/agoyal/cours/16*>.

Hammond, P.B., "Reverse Asset Allocation Alternatives at the Core", TIA-Cref Asset Management, Second Quarter, 2007.

Harloff, G.J., "Dynamic Asset Allocation; Beyond Buy-and-Hold", Technical Analysis of Stocks and Commodities Magazine, January 1998.

Harloff, G.J., "Harloff Capital Management's Market Outlook", October 2007.

Harloff, G.J., Eacott, E.E., "U.S. Business Cycle Math Quantification", Harloff Inc., <www.harloffcapital.com>, April 14, 2009, <*http://www.scribd.com/doc/14851834/US-Business-Cycle-Math-Quantification*>.

Harloff Inc., "Harloff's The Intelligent Fund Investor", Monthly Newsletter, 1993-2009.

Harloff Inc., "Harloff's The Intelligent Fund Investor", Vol. 12, Year 16, December 2009.

Hensel, C.R., Ezra, D.D., and Ilkiw, J.H., "The Importance of the Asset Allocation Decision," Financial Analysts Journal, 1991, 65-72.

Ibbotson, "Annual Returns 1926-1994", 1995.

Investment Company Institute, 2008.

Investor Economics Institute Analysis.

Investor Economics, 2005, 29.

Jeffrey, R.H., and Arnott, R.D. "Is your Alpha Big Enough to Cover Its Taxes?" The Journal of Portfolio Management, (Spring) 1993, 15-25.

Kapteyn, A., and Teppa, F. "Subjective Measures of Risk Aversion and Portfolio Choice", No. 2002-11, ISSN 0924-7815, CentER, Amsterdam, February 2002.

Laderman, J.M., "Mutual Funds: Can Anybody Out There Beat the S&P500?" Business Week, Dec. 17, 1998.

Leibowitz, M.L., and Hammond, P.B., "The Changing Mosaic of Investment Patterns", Journal of Portfolio Management, Spring 2004, vol. 30, no. 3, 10-25.

LIMRA International "Financial Situation of the Affluent", Opal Financial Group, 2002. <http://www.opalgroup.net/conferencehtml/2007/latin_private_wealth07/latin_am_private_wealth.php>.

Markowitz, H.M., "Portfolio Selection". Journal of Finance 7 (1), 1952, 77-91.

Markowitz, H.M., "Portfolio Selection". Ph.D. Thesis, University of Chicago, 1953

Markowitz, H.M., "The Optimization of a Quadratic Function Subject to Linear Constraints". Naval Research Logistics Quarterly 3, 1956, 111-133.

Markowitz, H. M., *Portfolio Selection: Efficient Diversification of Investments*, John Wiley & Sons, New Jersey,1959, (reprinted in 1970 by Yale University Press, *ISBN 978-0300013726*; second edition in 1991, Blackwell Publishing, *ISBN 978-1557861085*).

Martin, G.S., Puthenpurackal, J., "Imitation is the Sincerest Form of Flattery: Warren Buffett and Berkshire Hathaway"(August 13, 2005). Available at SSRN: <http://ssrn.com/abstract=806246>.

Meadors Investments, <http://www.meadorsinvestments.com>.

Michaud, R.O., "The Markowitz Optimization Enigma: Is Optimized Optimal?" Financial Analysts Journal, January-February 1989, 31-41.

Money Management Institute, 2003.

Money Management Institute, FRC, Press Release February 1, 2005, see Advisor Custom Publishing, Investment Advisor Magazine, August 2005.

Money Management Institute, Investment News, October 29, 2007.

Montecito Capital Management, <http://mcapitalmgt.com/html/assetallocation.htm>.

Muyot, M., "Fee-based 1", Oppenheimer Presentation, April 21, 2005. Opal Financial Group, 2007, <*http://www.opalgroup.net/conferencehtml/2007/latin_private_wealth07/latin_am_private_wealth.php*>. Partnervest Financial Group LLC, <*http://www.partnervest.com/Investment-Management-Services.html*>.

Producers Choice Generic Equity Index, "Upside Limits and Guarantees Vary With Specific Index Annuity Contracts," November 2007.

Sharpe, W. F., *Portfolio Theory and Capital Markets*, 1970, McGraw-Hill.

Sharpe, W. F., Goldstein, D. G., and Blythe, P.W., "The Distribution Builder: A Tool for Inferring Investor Preferences, Working Paper", Stanford University, 2000, <http://www.stanford.edu/~wfsharpe/art/qpaper/qpaper.html>.

Sjögren, K. H., "Overview and Trends in the Wealth Management Business", Investor Economics, CFA Institute, January 25, 2007. <*www.cfawebcasts.org*>.

Spectrem Group, see Barrons, November 12, 2007, 34.

Stine, B., and Lewis, J., "Guidelines for Rebalancing Passive-Investment Portfolios", J.

Financial Planning, April 1992, 80-86.

Sunguard, "A Profile of Asset Classes and Investments", Sunguard Broker and Investment Advisor, 2006 vol. 2, 6.

Taddingstone Consulting Group Inc., Canadian Millionaires Report, Toronto, ON M5J 1T1.

Tandem Financial Services, Inc. Study, 2003.

Thompson Financial Datastream, June 30, 2006.

Thorley, S.R., "The Time-Diversification Controversy", Financial Analysts Journal, May-
June 1995, 51, 68-76.

Wilcox, J., Horvitz, J., DiBartolomeo, D., "Investment Management for Taxable Private Investors," Research Foundation of CFA Institute, 2006.

World Wealth Report, 2006.

Zultowski, W.H., Phoenix High-Net Worth Market Insights, May 2007.

Zultowski, W.H., Phoenix High-Net Worth Market Insights, June 2007.

About the Author

Dr. Gary J. Harloff, Ph.D. is founder of Harloff Capital Management, a tactical money management specialist firm in Westlake, OH, a suburb of Cleveland, OH. Harloff Capital actively manages portfolios of funds, ETFs, for high net worth investors and an alternate investment fund for accredited investors. Dr. Harloff founded Harloff Inc. in 1981 to do stock market related research and registered his firm as an investment advisor in 1994. In his article *"Dynamic Asset Allocation: Beyond Buy-and-Hold"*, Technical Analysis of Stocks and Commodities magazine in January 1998, he illustrates how to beat the buy-and-hold strategy with dynamic asset allocation and introduces the dynamic frontier (time varying efficient frontier) concept. He has given investment lectures to groups in several states including: OH, MO, KY, FL, and Washington, DC.

His original stock market research began part-time in 1970 and continues today. His math modeling background led to the development of our new proprietary investment technology, not available on Wall or Main Street, to benefit our clients. He continues to have Harloff Capital Management manage his own portfolios along side of client portfolios. One of his original proprietary stock market indicators is the Harloff Value Index, HVI. This universal index quantifies investment opportunity in mutual funds, exchange traded funds, and indexes in many types of markets and countries. It is the basis for his monthly newsletter "Harloff's The Intelligent Fund Investor".

Prior to becoming a money manager, Dr. Harloff earned B.S., M.S., and Ph.D. degrees in Aerospace Engineering at University of Texas, Austin, University of Florida, Gainesville, and University of Texas, Arlington respectively. From 1968 to 1995 he worked in the aerospace/defense and energy industries and held DOD and DOE security clearances. From 1985 to 1995 he worked for NASA in the area of computational aerodynamics and propulsion in subsonic, supersonic, and hypersonic flight regimes. He developed technology for the Space Shuttle, future single-stage-to-orbit vehicles, air-breathing propulsion, and other systems. He specializes in computer simulation and modeling. He has two turbo-machinery patents. He has authored many engineering technical papers and presentations including two international technical presentations in Rome, Italy and Madrid, Spain. His disciplined and scientific training in aircraft and rocket science helps our investing process. Past performance does not insure future performance.

This page intentionally left blank.